PROOF

HOW TO KNOW
THE BOOK OF MORMON IS
∾TRUE∾

TOM G. ROSE

CFI
AN IMPRINT OF CEDAR FORT, INC.
SPRINGVILLE, UTAH

© 2011 Tom G. Rose
Illustrations by Mary Brickey Cole

ISBN 13: 978-1-59955-889-9

Published by CFI, an imprint of Cedar Fort, Inc., 2373 W. 700 S., Springville, UT 84663
Distributed by Cedar Fort, Inc. www.cedarfort.com

LIBRARY OF CONGRESS CATALOGING-IN-PUBLICATION DATA

Rose, Tom G., 1939- author.
  Proof : how to know the Book of Mormon is true / Tom G. Rose.
    pages cm
  Includes bibliographical references.
  ISBN 978-1-59955-889-9
  1. Book of Mormon--Evidences, authority, etc. 2. Revelation--Mormon Church. 3. Church of Jesus Christ of Latter-day Saints--Doctrines. I. Title.

  BX8627.R67 2011
  289.3'22--dc23

2011026790

Cover design by Angela D. Olsen
Cover design © 2011 by Lyle Mortimer
Edited and typeset by Melissa J. Caldwell

Printed in the United States of America

10 9 8 7 6 5 4 3 2 1

Printed on acid-free paper

*This book is a legacy of my life's experiences
with the sacred Book of Mormon,
and I dedicate it to my children and grandchildren,
and to all my posterity.*

CONTENTS

CONTENTS

INTRODUCTION

The Book of Mormon has been called the "keystone" of the Mormon religion. That singular statement underscores the fact that if the Book of Mormon is false, Joseph Smith is one of the greatest deceivers of all time. Therefore, the church he organized would also be false, because it would be man-made and not of divine origin.

If, on the other hand, the Book of Mormon is true, then Joseph Smith told the truth about what he saw, what he heard, and what he learned. Indeed, if the Book of Mormon is true, then Joseph Smith was a true prophet of God, and therefore, the church he organized is the only true church on earth. That church is The Church of Jesus Christ of Latter-day Saints, or, as it has been called because of the Book of Mormon, "The Mormon Church."

The Bible and the Book of Mormon are essential scriptural texts of The Church of Jesus Christ of Latter-day Saints. The Book of Mormon is a Second Witness with the Bible that Jesus Christ is the Son of God. Therefore, if the Book of Mormon is true, so is the Bible, and both stand as witnesses to the world that Jesus Christ is our Savior and Redeemer, and that each individual person *must* have faith in Him, repent of all sin, and obey His commandments or we cannot be saved in the Kingdom of God.

My purpose in writing this book is to present what I consider to be intellectual "proofs" that the Book of Mormon is sacred scripture—the word of God. After a lifetime of study, I am convinced that Joseph Smith could *not* have written the Book of Mormon, nor could any of his associates. To say otherwise suggests that the critic has not sincerely read the Book of Mormon. To those who have prayerfully studied it, as I have, has come a personal witness that the Book of Mormon is exactly what Joseph Smith said it is—the translation of an ancient record written by prophets who lived on the American continent from about 600 BC to around AD 420.

Over the past fifty years I have had an unusual relationship with the text of the Book of Mormon. Therefore, it is my desire to share some of the "proofs" I have discovered, and which I feel prove that the Book of Mormon is a sacred volume of divine scripture.

I begin with a brief description of the book's origin and contents. In 1823, at the age of seventeen, Joseph Smith declared that an angel of God showed him where a set of gold plates was buried with a sacred instrument called the Urim and Thummim. Please read Joseph's personal account and testimony found on three introductory pages at the beginning of the Book of Mormon, entitled "Testimony of the Prophet Joseph Smith." As you read his testimony ask yourself if it sounds made up or if it feels true. If you really want to know if the Book of Mormon is true, you will prayerfully read Joseph Smith's testimony.

Joseph testified that by the gift and inspiration of God, he translated those gold plates, which were engraved in Reformed Egyptian, into English. The result is a more than five hundred page book titled, *The Book of Mormon*. It was first published in Palmyra, New York, in 1830 when Joseph Smith was twenty-four years old.

The Book of Mormon chronicles the migration of two families from Jerusalem to America about 600 BC. You can read from 2 Kings 17:13–14, which describes conditions in Jerusalem about 600 BC when the Lord sent prophets to testify against Israel (see also 2 Chronicles 36:11–12, 15–17). The patriarch of one of these families was Lehi, a contemporary with the prophet Jeremiah. Lehi received a call from the Lord to warn the people of Jerusalem that if they did not repent, their city would be destroyed. Like most of the prophets of that time, Lehi was rejected. To save his life and the lives of his wife and children, Lehi was directed by the Lord to take his family and depart into the wilderness. They were joined by another family whose father was named Ishmael. The prophet Lehi led these families across the ocean to the Americas. Their descendants split into two groups, the Nephites and the Lamanites. The Nephites were led by prophets who recorded their religious history on gold plates.

The crowning event recorded in the Book of Mormon occurred in AD 34 when the more righteous part of the people were visited by the resurrected Jesus Christ, who organized His Church among them here in America, just as he had done in the Holy Land before his crucifixion.

After nearly two hundred years of peace, the people degenerated into a state of wickedness and in about AD 420, the last prophet—Mormon's son, Moroni—buried the sacred record of Lehi's descendants in a hill which is near the present day city of Palmyra in upstate New York.

If the Book of Mormon is in fact a sacred translation of gold plates that were recorded and compiled by ancient prophet-historians who lived on the American continent, then Joseph Smith was not only a true prophet but also one of the most important prophets of all time, the Book of Mormon is of supreme importance to every inhabitant on earth, Jesus Christ is the Savior and Redeemer of all mankind, and The Church of Jesus Christ of Latter-day Saints is the only true church on earth.

*(Note: From this point forward, every word printed in **bold type** is an actual quotation from the text of the Book of Mormon.)*

To help the reader understand my familiarity with the text of the Book of Mormon, I share the following personal biographical information:

In 1956–57, during my senior year in high school, I began attending early-morning seminary (an LDS religion class for high school–age youth) in Colton, California. I enjoyed it so much that I continued attending the next two years while enrolled as a student at San Bernardino Valley College. During 1958–59, the course of study for seminary was the Book of Mormon. Rita Miller, our seminary teacher, was an outstanding teacher with a strong testimony of the truthfulness of the Book of Mormon. Because of her testimony and my desire to know the truth, I read and studied the Book of Mormon and put Moroni's promise to the test. Moroni, the last prophet-historian in the Book of Mormon, declared, "**I would exhort you that when ye shall read these things . . . that ye would ask God, the Eternal Father, in the name of Christ, if these things are not true; and if ye shall ask with a sincere heart, with real intent, having faith in Christ, he will manifest the truth of it unto you, by the power of the Holy Ghost**" (Moroni 10:3–4). I sincerely wanted to know if the Book of Mormon was true, and so, as I read and studied it over a period of four to five months, I prayed often and asked God if the book was true. Finally, its truthfulness was manifest to me by the power of the Holy Ghost. I was amazed! I felt it in my whole being! I knew beyond any doubt that the Book of Mormon was true!

Having received this powerful witness, I felt compelled to share my testimony with others. Therefore, I submitted my mission application and was called to serve a full-time mission for the Church in the North Mexican Mission, headquartered in Monterrey, Mexico. For two and a half years, it was my privilege to go from house to house as a missionary, sweating in hundred-degree weather and testifying to everyone who would listen that Joseph Smith is a prophet, that the Book of Mormon is a true translation of an ancient record delivered to Joseph Smith by an angel of God, that Jesus Christ is the Savior and Redeemer of the world, and that The Church of Jesus Christ of Latter-day Saints is the Savior's restored Church. We had much success, and it was thrilling to baptize several people into the Church.

After my mission, I enrolled at Brigham Young University where I learned about the Church Education System and how I might become a full-time seminary teacher. If selected, it would be my privilege to teach high school age young people about the gospel of Jesus Christ as revealed in the Bible and the Book of Mormon. I completed the required training to become a seminary teacher, and after graduating from BYU with a Bachelors Degree and a secondary teaching certificate in 1964, I was grateful to be hired to teach seminary in the Church Education System. I taught at Bonneville High School and South Jr. and T. H. Bell Jr. Seminaries in Ogden, Utah, for six years. Every year, I taught the Book of Mormon course. I also taught the Old

Testament and Church History courses. In 1970, I made application, and was accepted, to participate in a summer workshop where we were taught how to write home study materials and actually began writing a Book of Mormon home study seminary course. At the end of that summer, I was hired as a full-time writer for Seminary Curriculum. In addition to writing the first Book of Mormon Home Study Seminary Course, we also wrote a new Book of Mormon outline for daily seminary teachers. In 1974, I decided to return to the classroom to teach seminary. I taught Book of Mormon at Hillcrest Seminary in Midvale, Utah, using the daily course I had helped write.

During the fall of 1975, Wayne Lynn, Director of the new Curriculum Department of the Church, asked me to join his staff as the Manager of Child Curriculum Development. I worked for the Church Curriculum Department for twenty-one years. During those years, among several other projects, it was my privilege to have significant input into the creation of the following:

1) *Book of Mormon Stories*—A guide for parents of young children to help them become familiar with major stories in the Book of Mormon and with Book of Mormon language. Our goal was to help prepare children to read the actual text of the Book of Mormon as they grew older.

2) *Primary 4 Book of Mormon Ages 8-11*—A Primary teacher's guide for teaching major stories from the Book of Mormon.

3) *The Guide to the Scriptures*—A scripture study aid for non-English editions of the Book of Mormon. Because of my familiarity with the text of the Book of Mormon, I was influential in adding hundreds of Book of Mormon references to this guide.

4) Footnotes for non-English editions of the Book of

Mormon—With the help of the computer, Roger Petersen (a coworker) and I evaluated every footnote in the English edition of the Book of Mormon to help decide which footnotes should be included in non-English editions. Only those which were principle oriented were retained.

5) Adult Book of Mormon Gospel Doctrine courses—Teachers' guides for teaching adults in Sunday School.

In 1996, I transferred from the Church Curriculum Department back to the Church Education System. I taught the Book of Mormon along with other courses at the Sandy Institute of Religion to college-age youth in south Salt Lake City. In 1997, my wife, Marilyn, and I were invited to move to northern California where I taught Institute and supervised early-morning seminary for four years. Here again, the Book of Mormon was an integral part of my work.

For the past forty to fifty years it has been my practice to read from the Book of Mormon as part of my personal daily scripture study. During these years of teaching and writing curriculum, I have also studied in detail the Bible, the Doctrine and Covenants, and the Pearl of Great Price. As I think back over my life, I have read the Book of Mormon from cover to cover at least fifty to sixty times in English and three or four times in Spanish, and spent hundreds of hours pouring over the text as I prepared lessons and wrote curriculum.

I believe I was given the privilege of writing curriculum and teaching Book of Mormon courses so often because of my testimony of its truthfulness and the ability I seem to have to see life applications throughout the book. It is my hope that my efforts over the years have helped some to desire to obtain their own personal testimonies of the truthfulness of the Book of Mormon by the power of the Holy Ghost. It is my sincere desire that each of my children and all my grandchildren will put forth the effort to obtain their own personal testimonies of its truthfulness by that same power and that they will make studying the Book of Mormon a lifetime pursuit. I know that anyone who desires to know the truth can come to know for him or herself that the Book of Mormon is true.

The Prophet Joseph Smith declared: "**I told the brethren that the Book of Mormon was the most correct of any book on earth, and the keystone of our religion, and a man would get nearer to God by abiding by its precepts, than by any other book**" (introduction to the Book of Mormon). I know from personal experience that this statement is true. If I qualify to return to God's presence, it will be in large part because of the influence the Book of Mormon has had in my personal life. It has helped me through a lifetime of challenges, including an eight-year bout with severe depression.

Because of the effect of the Book of Mormon in our lives, my wife and I decided to design our tombstone with the above statement by the Prophet Joseph Smith engraved on the back. Our tombstone has already been set in place at our final mortal resting place in Larkin Sunset Gardens in Sandy, Utah. Of course, it does not yet include the death dates.

Over these many years of reading, studying, and pondering the text of the Book of Mormon, I have often reflected on what I consider to be intellectual "proofs" of the authenticity of this book. I am convinced that it would have been absolutely impossible for Joseph Smith or any other person in the 1800s to write the Book of Mormon. I know by the power of the Holy Ghost that the Book of Mormon was translated by Joseph Smith from ancient records. The Book of Mormon comes from the same Divine Source as the

Bible. I have had the desire to record evidences I feel prove intellectually that the Book of Mormon is of divine origin. I invite you to prayerfully study the Book of Mormon and receive your own personal testimony of its truthfulness by the power of the Holy Ghost. I also hope the evidences presented in this book will help fortify your testimony of this sacred volume.

Tom G. Rose
August 2011

FOREWORD:
THE WORD OF GOD

Some may consider the word of God to be actual words that God Himself has spoken or given verbatim. A study of scripture reveals a more liberal definition.

Many people agree that the Bible contains the divine word of God. Within the Bible we find actual words spoken by the Father. For example, at the baptism of Jesus Christ a voice was heard from heaven declaring, "This is my beloved Son, in whom I am well pleased" (Matthew 3:17). In the Sermon on the Mount are recorded words spoken by Jesus as He taught the multitudes: "Blessed are the poor in spirit: for theirs is the kingdom of heaven" (Matthew 5:3).

Recorded scripture also contains the words of prophets. John the Baptist preached in the wilderness of Judea saying, "Repent ye: for the kingdom of heaven is at hand. For this is he that was spoken of by the prophet Esaias." Then, John the Baptist quoted the prophet Isaiah: "Prepare ye the way of the Lord" (see Matthew 3:2–3 and Isaiah 40:3).

The New Testament contains many letters written by the apostles to members of the Church: "Paul, an apostle of Jesus Christ by the will of God . . . to the saints and faithful brethren in Christ which are at Colosse" (Colossians 1:1–2).

Much of scripture is sacred historical narrative recorded by prophet-historians.

In summary, scripture contains the actual words of the Father, the actual words of Jesus Christ, the inspired words of prophets and apostles, along with sacred history recorded by prophet-historians. This explanation of the Word of God also holds true in the Book of Mormon. In other words, within the Book of Mormon you will encounter actual words spoken by Heavenly Father, and his divine Son, Jesus Christ, as well as recorded messages by true prophet-historians.

AUTHOR'S NOTE

Each chapter of this book contains what I consider to be proof that the Book of Mormon is of divine origin. I hope you have a strong desire to discover truth. Moses promised those of the latter days, "If . . . thou shalt seek the Lord thy God, thou shalt find him, if thou seek him with all thy heart and with all thy soul" (Deuteronomy 4:29). The Savior admonished each of us to "Ask, and it shall be given you; seek, and ye shall find; knock, and it shall be opened unto you: For every one that asketh receiveth; and he that seeketh findeth; and to him that knocketh it shall be opened" (Matthew 7:7–8).

Learning and applying truth take effort, but the rewards are priceless. I encourage you to prayerfully read and study that your effort may be rewarded with feelings of delicious discovery. You may study the chapters in order or skip around according to your personal interest, but I hope you will prayerfully study desiring to discover truth. These "proofs" are not meant to be comprehensive. Many more chapters could be added. Several books have been written showing archeological evidences, which confirm that an ancient civilization existed in America and corroborate many aspects of the Book of Mormon. A word-printing study was conducted by John L. Hilton and five of his associates (three non-LDS) that confirms "the view that different authors can be distinguished within the Book of Mormon, and that none is Joseph Smith or any of the other nineteenth-century candidates that have been proposed."[1]

Note

1. Noel B. Reynolds, ed., *Book of Mormon Authorship Revisited: The Evidence for Ancient Origins* (Provo, Utah: Foundation for Ancient Research and Mormon Studies, 1997), 11.

1

THE LIFE AND DEATH OF THE PROPHET JOSEPH SMITH

Throughout the vicinity of Palmyra, New York, where Joseph Smith lived as a boy, he was respected for his integrity and hard work ethic.

Mrs. Palmer, a lady advanced in years came to Utah with her daughter, who was a teacher in the Presbyterian schools of our state. . . . Mrs. Palmer's father, according to a story told by her, owned a farm near to that of the Smith family in New York. Her parents were friends of the Smith family, which she testified was one of the best in that locality, honest, religious, and industrious, but poor. . . . Mrs. Palmer said her father loved young Joseph Smith and often hired him to work with his boys. She was about six years old, she said, when he first came to their home. She remembered going into the field on an afternoon to play in the corn rows while her brothers worked. When evening came she was too tired to walk home and cried because her brothers refused to carry her. Joseph lifted her up to his shoulders and with his arm thrown across her feet to steady her and her arm about his neck he carried her to their home. . . . She stated that one of their church leaders came to her father to remonstrate against allowing such close friendship between his family and the "Smith boy," as he called him. Her father, she said, defended his own position by saying that the boy was the best help he had ever found. He told the churchman that he always fixed the time of hoeing his large field to that when he could secure the services of Joseph Smith, because of the influence that boy had over the wild boys of the neighborhood, and explained that when these boys worked by themselves much time would be spent in arguing and quarreling, which often ended in a ring fight. But when Joseph Smith worked with them the work went steadily forward, and he got the full worth of the wages he paid.[1]

Joseph was an honest boy, so it was easy for his parents and eight brothers and sisters to believe he told the truth regarding his visions and the gold plates. Joseph's mother, Lucy Mack Smith, recorded: "Every evening we gathered our children together. I think that we presented the most peculiar aspect of any family that ever lived upon the earth, all seated in a circle, father, mother, sons, and daughters listening in breathless anxiety to the religious teachings of a boy [seventeen] years of age. . . .

"We were convinced that God was about to bring to light something that we might stay our minds upon, something that we could get a more definite idea of than anything which had been taught us heretofore, and we rejoiced in it with exceeding great joy. . . . No jar nor discord disturbed our peace, and tranquility reigned in our midst."[2]

Orrin Porter Rockwell was a pioneer from the day that Joseph received his first vision or visitation by holy beings; from his own statement made to me [Elizabeth Roundy] in 1875 when he came to me to write the history of his life. He stated that Joseph Smith's father and mother used to come to his father's house and tell his parents of the wonderful things that were being revealed to their son Joseph. He said he used to watch for their coming and plead with his mother to let him stay up to keep the pine torch burning, as that was the only means they used to illuminate their dwelling. When they spoke of getting means to print the Book of Mormon Porter determined to help, and as he had no other way he went after his day's work was done and picked berries by moonlight and in the early morning and sold the berries and gave Joseph the money to help with the printing. He also gathered wood [and] hauled it to town and sold it and used the means for the same purpose. No man loved Joseph the Prophet more than O. P. Rockwell. He was not one having the advantage of education but his heart was devoted to the cause of truth. He would not have hesitated to have given his life for Joseph at any time.[3]

The firsthand accounts of hundreds of persons who had personal contact with Joseph Smith are recorded in the more than four hundred pages of the book *Remembering Joseph*, by Mark L. McConkie. The following is found on pages 105–106:

> Mary A. Lambert—"I first saw Joseph Smith in the spring of 1843. When the boat in which we came up the Mississippi River reached the landing at Nauvoo, several of the leading brethren were there to meet the company of Saints that had come on it. Among those brethren was the Prophet Joseph Smith. I knew him the instant my eyes rested on him, and at that moment I received my testimony that he was a prophet of God, for I never had such a feeling for mortal man as thrilled my being when my eyes first rested upon Joseph Smith. He was not pointed out to me. I knew him from all other men, and, child that I was (I was only fourteen), I knew that I saw a prophet of God."

Someone has said, "O that mine enemy would write a book." Why would anyone want his enemy to write a book?

If a person writes a book, they open themselves to criticism. But to say, "Thus saith the Lord," or to claim to bring forth new scripture to the world, opens Joseph Smith to serious critique by theologians and the most noted religionists of the world. Ever since the Book of Mormon was published in 1830, critics have tried in vain to find fault with its text. Any person who takes away from the Prophet Joseph Smith his divine, prophetic gifts, needs to account in some other way for the origin of the Book of Mormon.

Long after the Saints had moved west, the Prophet's wife, Emma, held strong to her belief in the divine origin of the Book of Mormon. She told her son,

> My belief is that the Book of Mormon is of divine authenticity—I have not the slightest doubt of it. I am satisfied that no man could have dictated the writing of the manuscript unless he was inspired; for, when [I was] acting as his scribe, your father would dictate to me hour after hour; and when returning after meals, or after interruptions, he would at once begin where he had left off, without either seeing the manuscript or having any portion of it read to him. It would have been improbable that a learned man could do this; and, for one so ignorant and unlearned as he was, it was simply impossible.[4]

But the Book of Mormon is not the only book of scripture that came through the Prophet Joseph Smith. After completing the translation of the Book of Mormon, the Prophet was commanded to make an inspired translation of the Bible. This work is called the Inspired Version of the Bible and is indeed a wonderful aid for serious Bible students. The Book of Moses in the Pearl of Great Price is an excerpt from the Inspired Version. Could an evil charlatan, as some critics have called Joseph, make corrections to the text of the Bible which not only make sense, but actually help in understanding its message? (See Chapter 10—Isaiah passages in the Book of Mormon.) And if such corrections were attempted illicitly, could not biblical scholars expose him?

In July 1835, Michael H. Chandler came to Kirtland, Ohio, to exhibit some Egyptian mummies and scrolls that contained hieroglyphic writings. Some members of the Church purchased the scrolls, and the Prophet Joseph translated them and discovered that they were writings of Abraham which he had recorded while in Egypt. The Book of Abraham in the Pearl of Great Price contains priceless truths recorded by the great patriarch Abraham with two facsimiles copied from the scrolls themselves. These seven and one-half pages of scripture add, heretofore, unknown truths about the life of the great patriarch Abraham. Study these passages carefully. If they are not the translation of "ancient records," what is their origin?

The book of Doctrine and Covenants is modern scripture and contains 138 sections, of which 134 of these are prophetic declarations by the Prophet Joseph Smith. The "Explanatory Introduction" at the first of the book, describes the contents of the Doctrine and Covenants as follows: "In the revelations, one hears the tender but firm voice of the Lord Jesus Christ, speaking anew in the dispensation of the fulness of times." These sacred additions to the scriptures are further written evidence of the prophetic call of Joseph Smith and of the divinity of the Book of Mormon.

At the age of thirty-eight on his way to Carthage to meet a martyr's death, Joseph said: "I am going like a lamb to the slaughter; but I am as calm as a summer's morning; I have a conscience void of offence towards God, and towards all men" (D&C 135:4).

On October 4, 2009, Elder Jeffrey R. Holland of the

Quorum of the Twelve Apostles declared:

> May I refer to a modern 'last days' testimony? When Joseph Smith and his brother Hyrum started for Carthage to face what they knew would be an imminent martyrdom, Hyrum read these words to comfort the heart of his brother: '**Thou hast been faithful; wherefore . . . thou shalt be made strong, even unto the sitting down in the place which I have prepared in the mansions of my Father. And now I, Moroni, bid farewell . . . until we shall meet before the judgment-seat of Christ.**'
>
> A few short verses from the 12th chapter of Ether in the Book of Mormon. Before closing the book, Hyrum turned down the corner of the page from which he had read, marking it as part of the everlasting testimony for which these two brothers were about to die. I hold in my hand that book, the very copy from which Hyrum read, the same corner of the page turned down, still visible. Later, when actually incarcerated in the jail, *Joseph the Prophet turned to the guards who held him captive and bore a powerful testimony of the divine authenticity of the Book of Mormon. Shortly thereafter pistol and ball would take the lives of these two testators.*[5]

Then, Elder Holland bore his powerful testimony:

> I ask that my testimony of the Book of Mormon and all that it implies, given today under my own oath and office, be recorded by men on earth and angels in heaven . . . I want it absolutely clear when I stand before the judgment bar of God that I declared to the world, in the most straightforward language I could summon, that the Book of Mormon is true, that it came forth the way Joseph said it came forth and was given to bring happiness and hope to the faithful in the travail of the latter days.[6]

John Taylor, who was in Carthage Jail at the time of the

martyrdom, and was an eyewitness, recorded the following:

> To seal the testimony of this book and the Book of Mormon, we announce the martyrdom of Joseph Smith the Prophet, and Hyrum Smith the Patriarch. They were shot in Carthage jail, on the 27th of June, 1844, about five o'clock p.m., by an armed mob—painted black—of from 150 to 200 persons. . .
>
> John Taylor and Willard Richards, two of the Twelve, were the only persons in the room at the time; the former was wounded in a savage manner with four balls, but has since recovered; the latter, through the providence of God, escaped, without even a hole in his robe.
>
> Joseph Smith, the Prophet and Seer of the Lord, has done more, save Jesus only, for the salvation of men in this world, than any other man that ever lived in it. In the short space of twenty years, he has brought forth the Book of Mormon, which he translated by the gift and power of God, and has been the means of publishing it on two continents; has sent the fulness of the everlasting gospel, which it contained, to the four quarters of the earth; has brought forth the revelations and commandments which compose this book of Doctrine and Covenants, and many other wise documents and instructions for the benefit of the children of men; gathered many thousands of the Latter-day Saints, founded a great city, and left a fame and name that cannot be slain. He lived great, and he died great in the eyes of God and his people; and like most of the Lord's anointed in ancient times, has sealed his mission and his works with his own blood; and so has his brother Hyrum. (D&C 135:1–3)

Here, we see the divine Law of Witnesses in operation. (See Chapter 2.) Two witnesses were martyred and two witnesses saw their martyrdom.

How can anyone believe that a man of such great

integrity and devotion could perpetrate such a falsehood claiming that God and angels appeared unto him, that he was a prophet of God, and that under divine inspiration he translated a sacred record and organized the true Church of Jesus Christ? A more logical conclusion is that Joseph Smith was an honest person, and that he did what he said he did!

Notes

1. Mark L. McConkie, ed., *Remembering Joseph: Personal Recollections of Those Who Knew the Prophet Joseph Smith* (Salt Lake City: Deseret Book, 2003), 27–28.
2. Lucy Mack Smith, "*The History of Lucy Smith, Mother of the Prophet*," 1844–45 manuscript, book 4, p. 1, Church Archives, as quoted in *Teachings of the Presidents of the Church: Joseph Smith* (Salt Lake City: The Church of Jesus Christ of Latter-day Saints, 2007), 486.
3. McConkie, *Remembering Joseph*, 299.
4. Ibid., 303.
5. Jeffrey R. Holland, "Safety for the Soul," *Ensign*, Nov. 2009, 89; emphasis added.
6. Ibid., 90.

∽ 2 ∽

THE DIVINE LAW
OF WITNESSES

God Himself has established the divine Law of Witnesses. God gives us proof that his word is true, but leaves it up to us to decide for ourselves whether or not we will believe and obey the truth. This divine law is manifest throughout the Bible and in all scripture. In the Bible, in the book of Deuteronomy, the Law of Witnesses was given as part of the Mosaic code: "At the mouth of two witnesses, or at the mouth of three witnesses, shall the matter be established" (Deuteronomy 19:15). In the New Testament Paul wrote: "In the mouth of two or three witnesses shall every word be established" (2 Corinthians 13:1).

In the Book of Mormon, Nephi applied the Law of Witnesses as proof that his words were true:

> **I, Nephi, write more of the words of Isaiah, for my soul delighteth in his words. For I will liken his words unto my people, and I will send them forth unto all my children, for he verily saw my Redeemer, even as I have seen him. And my brother, Jacob, also has seen him as I have seen him; wherefore, I will send their words forth unto my children to _prove_ unto them that my words are true. Wherefore, by**

the words of three, God hath said, I will establish
my word. Nevertheless, God sendeth more witnesses,
and he *proveth* all his words (2 Nephi 11:2–3; italics
added).

The Law of Witnesses is complied with by the following
testimonies which are printed in every copy of the Book of
Mormon:

THE TESTIMONY OF THREE WITNESSES

Be it known unto all nations, kindreds, tongues,
and people, unto whom this work shall come: That
we, through the grace of God the Father, and our Lord
Jesus Christ, have seen the plates which contain this
record, which is a record of the people of Nephi, and
also of the Lamanites, their brethren, and also of the
people of Jared, who came from the tower of which
hath been spoken. And we also know that they have
been translated by the gift and power of God, for his
voice hath declared it unto us; wherefore we know
of a surety that the work is true. And we also testify that we have seen the engravings which are upon
the plates; and they have been shown unto us by the
power of God, and not of man. And we declare with
words of soberness, that an angel of God came down
from heaven, and he brought and laid before our eyes,
that we beheld and saw the plates, and the engravings
thereon; and we know that it is by the grace of God
the Father, and our Lord Jesus Christ, that we beheld
and bear record that these things are true. And it is
marvelous in our eyes. Nevertheless, the voice of the
Lord commanded us that we should bear record of it;
wherefore, to be obedient unto the commandments of

God, we bear testimony of these things. And we know that if we are faithful in Christ, we shall rid our garments of the blood of all men, and be found spotless before the judgment-seat of Christ, and shall dwell with him eternally in the heavens. And the honor be to the Father, and to the Son, and to the Holy Ghost, which is one God. Amen.

OLIVER COWDERY
DAVID WHITMER
MARTIN HARRIS

Each of these men was excommunicated from the church. However, none of them ever denied seeing the angel and the gold plates. Later in life Oliver Cowdery and Martin Harris came back to the Church and were re-baptized. The fact that they were both disgruntled with the Prophet Joseph Smith and the Church, but continued to be true to their testimonies strengthens the value of their witness of the Book of Mormon. On their deathbeds they both bore powerful testimonies of seeing the angel and the gold plates.

During the last year of his life, David Whitmer published his final testimony in a seventy-five page booklet:

> I will say once more to all mankind, that I have never at any time denied that testimony or any part thereof. I also testify to the world, that neither Oliver Cowdery or Martin Harris, ever at any time denied their testimony. They both died reaffirming the truth of the divine authenticity of the Book of Mormon. I was present at the deathbed of Oliver Cowdery, and his last words were, 'Brother David, be true to your testimony to the Book of Mormon.' He died here in Richmond, Missouri, on March 3d, 1850.[1]

THE TESTIMONY OF EIGHT WITNESSES

Be it known unto all nations, kindreds, tongues, and people, unto whom this work shall come: That Joseph Smith, Jun., the translator of this work, has shown unto us the plates of which hath been spoken, which have the appearance of gold; and as many of the leaves as the said Smith has translated we did handle with our hands; and we also saw the engravings thereon, all of which has the appearance of ancient work, and of curious workmanship. And this we bear record with words of soberness, that the said Smith has shown unto us, for we have seen and hefted, and know of a surety that the said Smith has got the plates of which we have spoken. And we give our names unto the world, to witness unto the world that which we have seen. And we lie not, God bearing witness of it.

CHRISTIAN WHITMER	**HIRAM PAGE**
JACOB WHITMER	**JOSEPH SMITH, SEN.**
PETER WHITMER, JUN.	**HYRUM SMITH**
JOHN WHITMER	**SAMUEL H. SMITH**

"The lives of the eleven witnesses are well documented; each was questioned closely about his natural and supernatural experiences. The documents on their lives and testimonies are so numerous that they could fill volumes."[2]

John Whitmer responded in writing several times to inquiries about his testimony of the Book of Mormon.

Two years before his death, dating the letter 5 March 1876, John wrote: "Oliver Cowdery lived in Richmond, Mo., some 40 miles from here, at the time of his death. I went to see him and was with him for several days previous to his demise. . . . I have never heard that any one of the three or eight witnesses ever denied the testimony that they have borne to the Book as published in the first edition of the Book of Mormon. . . . Our names have gone forth to all nations, tongues, and people as a divine revelation from God."[3]

The Prophet Joseph Smith's own words about the coming forth of the Book of Mormon are:

TESTIMONY OF THE PROPHET JOSEPH SMITH

On the evening of the . . . twenty-first of September [1823] . . . I betook myself to prayer and supplication to Almighty God. . . .

While I was thus in the act of calling upon God, I discovered a light appearing in my room, which continued to increase until the room was lighter than at noonday, when immediately a personage appeared at my bedside, standing in the air, for his feet did not touch the floor.

He had on a loose robe of most exquisite whiteness. It was a whiteness beyond anything earthly I had ever seen; nor do I believe that any earthly thing could be made to appear so exceedingly white and brilliant. His hands were naked, and his arms also, a little above the wrists; so, also, were his feet naked, as were his legs, a little above the ankles. His head and neck were also bare. I could discover that he had no other clothing on but this robe, as it was open, so that I could see into his bosom.

Not only was his robe exceedingly white, but his whole person was glorious beyond description, and his countenance truly like lightning. The room was exceedingly light, but not so very bright as immediately around his person. When I first looked upon him, I was afraid; but the fear soon left me.

He called me by name, and said unto me that he was a messenger sent from the presence of God to me, and that his name was Moroni; that God had a work for me to do; and that my name should be had for good and evil among all nations, kindreds, and tongues, or that it should be both good and evil spoken of among all people.

He said there was a book deposited, written upon gold plates, giving an account of the former inhabitants of this continent, and the source from whence they sprang. He also said that the fulness of the everlasting Gospel was contained in it, as delivered by the Savior to the ancient inhabitants;

Also, that there were two stones in silver bows—and these stones, fastened to a breastplate, constituted what is called the Urim and Thummim—deposited with the plates; and the possession and use of these stones were what constituted *Seers* in ancient or former times; and that God had prepared them for the purpose of translating the book.

* * * * * *

Again, he told me, that when I got those plates of which he had spoken—for the time that they should be obtained was not yet fulfilled—I should not show them to any person; neither the breastplate with the Urim and Thummim; only to those to whom I should be commanded to show them; if I did I should be destroyed. While he was conversing with me about the plates, the vision was opened to my mind that I could see the place where the plates were deposited, and that so clearly and distinctly that I knew the place again when I visited it.

After this communication, I saw the light in the room

begin to gather immediately around the person of him who had been speaking to me, and it continued to do so, until the room was again left dark, except just around him, when instantly I saw, as it were, a conduit open right up into heaven, and he ascended until he entirely disappeared, and the room was left as it had been before this heavenly light had made its appearance.

I lay musing on the singularity of the scene, and marveling greatly at what had been told to me by this extraordinary messenger; when, in the midst of my meditation, I suddenly discovered that my room was again beginning to get lighted, and in an instant, as it were, the same heavenly messenger was again by my bedside.

He commenced, and again related the very same things which he had done at his first visit, without the least variation; which having done, he informed me of great judgments which were coming upon the earth, with great desolations by famine, sword, and pestilence; and that these grievous judgments would come on the earth in this generation. Having related these things, he again ascended as he had done before.

By this time, so deep were the impressions made on my mind, that sleep had fled from my eyes, and I lay overwhelmed in astonishment at what I had both seen and heard. But what was my surprise when again I beheld the same messenger at my bedside, and heard him rehearse or repeat over again to me the same things as before; and added a caution to me, telling me that Satan would try to tempt me (in consequence of the indigent circumstances of my father's family), to get the plates for the purpose of getting rich. This he forbade me, saying that I must have no other object in view in getting the plates but to glorify God, and must not be influenced by any other motive than that of building His kingdom; otherwise I could not get them.

After this third visit, he again ascended into heaven as before, and I was again left to ponder on the strangeness of what I had just experienced; when almost immediately after the heavenly messenger had ascended from me the third time, the cock crowed, and I found that day was approaching, so that our interviews must have occupied the whole of that night.

I shortly after arose from my bed, and, as usual, went to the necessary labors of the day; but, in attempting to work as at other times, I found my strength so exhausted as to render me entirely unable. My father, who was laboring along with me, discovered something to be wrong with me, and told me to go home. I started with the intention of going to the house; but, in attempting to cross the fence out of the field where we were, my strength entirely failed me, and I fell helpless on the ground, and for a time was quite unconscious of anything.

The first thing that I can recollect was a voice speaking unto me, calling me by name. I looked up, and beheld the same messenger standing over my head, surrounded by light as before. He then again related unto me all that he had related to me the previous night, and commanded me to go to my father and tell him of the vision and commandments which I had received.

I obeyed; I returned to my father in the field, and rehearsed the whole matter to him. He replied to me that it was of God, and told me to go and do as commanded by the messenger. I left the field, and went to the place where the messenger had told me the plates were deposited; and owing to the distinctness of the vision which I had had concerning it, I knew the place the instant that I arrived there.

Convenient to the village of Manchester, Ontario county, New York, stands a hill of considerable size, and the most elevated of any in the neighborhood. On the west side of this hill, not far from the top, under a stone of considerable size, lay the plates, deposited in a stone box. This stone was thick and rounding in the middle on the upper side, and thinner towards the edges, so that the middle part of it was visible above the ground, but the edge all around was covered with earth.

Having removed the earth, I obtained a lever, which I got fixed under the edge of the stone, and with a little exertion raised it up. I looked in, and there indeed did I behold the plates, the Urim and Thummim, and the breastplate, as stated by the messenger. The box in which they lay was formed by laying stones together in some kind of cement. In the bottom of the box were laid two stones crossways of the box, and on these stones lay the plates and the other things with them.

I made an attempt to take them out, but was forbidden by the messenger, and was again informed that the time for bringing them forth had not yet arrived, neither would it, until four years from that time; but he told me that I should come to that place precisely in one year from that time, and that he would there meet with me, and that I should continue to do so until the time should come for obtaining the plates.

Accordingly, as I had been commanded, I went at the end of each year, and at each time I found the same messenger there, and received instruction and intelligence from him at each of our interviews, respecting what the

Lord was going to do, and how and in what manner His kingdom was to be conducted in the last days.

* * * * * *

At length the time arrived for obtaining the plates, the Urim and Thummim, and the breastplate. On the twenty-second day of September, one thousand eight hundred and twenty-seven, having gone as usual at the end of another year to the place where they were deposited, the same heavenly messenger delivered them up to me with this charge: That I should be responsible for them; that if I should let them go carelessly, or through any neglect of mine, I should be cut off; but that if I would use all my endeavors to preserve them, until he, the messenger, should call for them, they should be protected.

I soon found out the reason why I had received such strict charges to keep them safe, and why it was that the messenger had said that when I had done what was required at my hand, he would call for them. For no sooner was it known that I had them, than the most strenuous exertions were used to get them from me. Every stratagem that could be invented was resorted to for that purpose. The persecution became more bitter and severe than before, and multitudes were on the alert continually to get them from me if possible. But by the wisdom of God, they remained safe in my hands, until I had accomplished by them what was required at my hand. When, according to arrangements, the messenger called for them, I delivered them up to him; and he has them in his charge until this day, being the second day of May, one thousand eight hundred and thirty-eight." (See Joseph Smith—History, Pearl of Great Price, and

History of The Church of Jesus Christ of Latter-day Saints, vol. 1, chapters 1 through 6.)

Joseph Smith's whole life from his first vision in 1820 at the age of fourteen to his martyrdom on June 27, 1844, at the age of thirty-seven, was a witness to the truthfulness of the Book of Mormon and his divine calling as a prophet. Joseph's final testimony as explained above by Elder Jeffrey R. Holland was given to his guards in Carthage Jail shortly before he sealed his testimony with his own blood.

Every one of these witnesses was true to his testimony until death.

In a court of law, two witnesses are usually all that is needed to establish truth. With the Book of Mormon we have eleven eyewitnesses of the sacred gold plates, in addition to the witness of the Prophet Joseph Smith.

Notes

1. Richard L. Anderson, "Personal Writings of the Book of Mormon Witnesses," in Reynolds, *Book of Mormon Authorship Revisited: The Evidence for ancient Origins* (Provo: Foundation for Ancient Research and Mormon Studies, 1997), 50.
2. Ibid., 40.
3. Ibid., 55–56.

3

THE DIVINITY OF JESUS CHRIST AND HIS ATONEMENT

The subtitle of the Book of Mormon is "**Another Testament of Jesus Christ**." The Old Testament in the Bible contains prophesies of the birth, ministry, and crucifixion of Jesus Christ. Then in the New Testament are found four eyewitness accounts of the fulfillment of the Old Testament prophesies, making the Bible a powerful testament that Jesus of Nazareth is indeed the Savior of the world. The Book of Mormon contains numerous, inspired prophecies and testimonies of the birth, ministry, and atoning sacrifice of Jesus Christ, as well as the account of the visit of the resurrected Jesus Christ in ancient America shortly after His ascension in Jerusalem, and thus fulfills the law of witnesses by joining the Bible as "**Another Testament of Jesus Christ**."

The Book of Mormon is full of prophecies of the Savior's life and mission. Consider the following powerful statements of the divinity of Jesus Christ.

Between 600 and 592 BC, Nephi recorded a vision he had of the birth and baptism of the Savior:

I looked and beheld the great city of Jerusalem,

and also other cities. And I beheld the city of Nazareth; and in the city of Nazareth I beheld a virgin, and she was exceedingly fair and white. . . . And the angel said unto me: Behold the Lamb of God, yea, even the Son of the Eternal Father! . . . And I looked, and beheld the Son of God going forth among the children of men; and I saw many fall down at his feet and worship him. . . . And I looked and beheld the Redeemer of the world, of whom my father had spoken; and I also beheld the prophet who should prepare the way before him. And the Lamb of God went forth and was baptized of him; and after he was baptized, I beheld the heavens open, and the Holy Ghost come down out of heaven and abide upon him in the form of a dove. (1 Nephi 11:13, 21, 24, 27)

Nephi also witnessed the Savior's ministry and His crucifixion:

And I beheld that he went forth ministering unto the people, in power and great glory; and the multitudes were gathered together to hear him; and I beheld that they cast him out from among them. And I also beheld twelve others following him. . . . And I looked, and I beheld the Lamb of God going forth among the children of men. And I beheld multitudes of people who were sick, and who were afflicted with all manner of diseases, and with devils and unclean spirits; and the angel spake and showed all these things unto me. And they were healed by the power of the Lamb of God; and the devils and the unclean spirits were cast out. . . . And I looked and beheld the Lamb of God, that he was taken by the people; yea, the Son of the everlasting God was judged of the world. . . . And I, Nephi, saw that he was lifted up upon the cross and slain for the sins of the world. (1 Nephi 11:28–29, 31–33)

In addition to this amazing prophecy of the ministry and crucifixion of the Savior, Nephi also recorded a masterful testimony by his younger brother Jacob in 2 Nephi 9. This chapter contains 54 verses and beautifully explains how the "**infinite atonement**" ransoms mankind from the Fall of Adam and Eve.

O how great the goodness of our God, who prepareth a way for our escape from the grasp of this awful monster; yea, that monster, death and hell, which I call the death of the body, and also the death of the spirit. . . . O the greatness of the mercy of our God, the Holy One of Israel! For he delivereth his saints from that awful monster the devil, and death, and hell . . . which is endless torment. . . . And he cometh into the world that he may save all men if they will hearken unto his voice; for behold, he suffereth the pains of all men . . . who belong to the family of Adam. And he suffereth this that the resurrection might pass upon all men, that all might stand before him at the great and judgment day. And he commandeth all men that they must repent, and be baptized in his name, having perfect faith in the Holy One of Israel, or they cannot be saved in the kingdom of God. . . . O, my beloved brethren, turn away from your sins; shake off the chains of him that would bind you fast; come unto that God who is the rock of your salvation. (2 Nephi 9:10, 19, 21–23, 45)

Repeated readings of 2 Nephi 9 with sincere prayer and pondering could motivate a grievous sinner to repent and receive mercy and forgiveness through the Atonement of Jesus Christ. Elder Joseph Fielding Smith called Jacob's discourse, "One of the most enlightening discourses ever delivered in regard to the atonement. . . . It should be carefully read by every person seeking salvation."[1]

The first four hundred pages of the Book of Mormon contain the prophecies of more than a dozen different prophets who testified of the birth and saving Atonement of Jesus Christ. Consider the specificity of the following prophecy given by Nephi, given around 545 BC, shortly before his death: "**There is save one Messiah spoken of by the prophets, and that Messiah is he who should be rejected of the Jews. For according to the words of the prophets, the Messiah cometh in six hundred years from the time that my father left Jerusalem; and according to the words of the prophets, and also the word of the angel of God, his name shall be Jesus Christ, the Son of God**" (2 Nephi 25:18–19).

How could it be clearer? To help us understand how important the knowledge of the Savior was to Nephi and his people, he explained: "**We labor diligently to write, to persuade our children, and also our brethren, to believe in Christ. . . . And we talk of Christ, we rejoice in Christ, we preach of Christ, we prophesy of Christ, and we write according to our prophecies, that our children may know to what source they may look for a remission of their sins**" (2 Nephi 25:23, 26).

Various Book of Mormon prophets prophesied and bore testimony of the Atonement of Jesus Christ from hundreds of years before the Savior's birth right up to 5 BC:

- *Enos*—Between 544 and 421 BC (Enos 1:26–27)
- *Amaleki*—Between 279 and 130 BC (Omni 1:26)
- *King Benjamin*—About 124 BC (Mosiah 3:5–8, 17)
- *Abinadi*—About 150 BC (Mosiah 16:6–13)
- *Alma the Elder*—Between 100 and 92 BC (Mosiah 26:22–26—words of the Savior)
- *Alma the Younger*—Between 83–73 BC (Alma 5:48; 7:7–14; 34:4–8; 36:17–20)

- *Aaron*—About 90 BC (Alma 22:12–14)
- *Helaman, son of Helaman*—About 30 BC (Helaman 5:9–12)
- *Samuel the Lamanite*—5 BC (Helaman 14:2–8)

The Book of Mormon contains the sacred account of the visit of the resurrected Jesus Christ to the inhabitants of ancient America, after his crucifixion and resurrection in Jerusalem. The following was recorded by another prophet named Nephi, who lived on the American continent in AD 34, as he related the account of a group of people gathered in the land called Bountiful:

> They heard a voice as if it came out of heaven . . . and it said unto them: Behold my Beloved Son, in whom I am well pleased, in whom I have glorified my name—hear ye him. And it came to pass, as they understood they cast their eyes up again towards heaven; and behold, they saw a Man descending out of heaven; and he was clothed in a white robe; and he came down and stood in the midst of them; and the eyes of the whole multitude were turned upon him. . . . And it came to pass that he stretched forth his hand and spake unto the people, saying: Behold, I am Jesus Christ, whom the prophets testified shall come into the world. . . . And it came to pass that the multitude went forth, and thrust their hands into his side, and did feel the prints of the nails in his hands and in his feet; and this they did do, going forth one by one until they had all gone forth, and did see with their eyes and did feel with their hands, and did know of a surety and did bear record, that it was he, of whom it was written by the prophets, that should come. And when they had all gone forth and had witnessed for themselves, they did cry out with one accord, saying: Hosanna! Blessed be the name of the

Most High God! And they did fall down at the feet of Jesus, and did worship him. (3 Nephi 11:3, 6–10, 15–17.)

The resurrected Christ then taught these people his gospel, called twelve special witnesses, gave them power and authority to baptize, organized His Church, instituted the sacrament, and ministered among the people for three days. Third Nephi chapters 12–30 is the account of the resurrected Christ's ministry among the Nephites in America in AD 34. Third Nephi contains the actual teachings of the resurrected Christ and may be referred to as the fifth Gospel, along with Matthew, Mark, Luke, and John.

Following the Savior's ministry in America the people enjoyed, an unprecedented, millennial-like era that lasted for nearly two hundred years. The four-page book of Fourth Nephi is a brief account of this peaceful time during which **"there was no contention in the land, because of the love of God which did dwell in the hearts of the people. And there were no envyings, nor strifes, nor tumults, nor whoredoms, nor lyings, nor murders, nor any manner of lasciviousness; and surely there could not be a happier people among all the people who had been created by the hand of God"** (4 Nephi 1:15–16).

The prophet Mormon lived about AD 310–385. At age ten, he was recognized as a serious-minded youth, and at age fifteen he became a military leader among the Nephites. Mormon was selected by the Lord to make an abridgment of the sacred history of his people and was the principle recorder of the gold plates from which the Book of Mormon was translated. Mormon was a great prophet and witnessed the downfall of his people. He prophesied that the record he made on plates of gold would be brought to light in the latter days. Of this record, Mormon declared, **"Now these**

things are written . . . to be hid up unto the Lord that
they may come forth in his own due time . . . they shall
come forth according to the commandment of the Lord.
And behold, they shall go unto the unbelieving of the
Jews; and for this intent shall they go—that they may be
persuaded that Jesus is the Christ, the Son of the living
God . . . unto the fulfilling of his covenant; and also that
the seed of this people may more fully believe his gospel"
(Mormon 5:12–15).

Mormon's son, Moroni, the last of the Book of Mormon
prophets, recorded his testimony of Jesus Christ before burying the plates in the hill Cumorah: "**Come unto Christ,
and be perfected in him, and deny yourselves of all
ungodliness, and love God with all your might, mind
and strength, then is his grace sufficient for you, that by
his grace ye may be perfect in Christ**" (Moroni 10:32).

"The principal and commanding figure in the Book of
Mormon, from first chapter to last, is the Lord Jesus Christ.
In its unparalleled focus on the Messianic message of the
Savior of the world, the Book of Mormon is rightly referred
to as . . . 'another testament' of Jesus Christ."[2]

The Book of Mormon testifies of the redeeming power
of the Atonement by relating accounts of the change of heart
experienced by the "**most vile**" of sinners. The list includes
Alma the Elder, Alma the Younger, the four sons of king
Mosiah, king Lamoni's father, and Zeezrom, a wicked
lawyer.

ALMA THE ELDER

Alma the Elder was a wicked priest in the court of king
Noah who ruled in wickedness. "**And he had many wives
and concubines. And he did cause his people to commit
sin, and do that which was abominable in the sight of**

the Lord. Yea, and they did commit whoredoms and all manner of wickedness. . . . For he put down all the priests that had been consecrated by his father, and consecrated new ones in their stead, such as were lifted up in the pride of their hearts" (Mosiah 11:2, 5).

Alma was one of the wicked priests of king Noah who spoke "lying and vain words to his people" and spent "their time with harlots" (Mosiah 11:11, 14). The prophet Abinadi came among the people, calling them to repentance and warning them of imminent bondage and even destruction if they did not repent. Abinadi was taken into custody and the wicked priests questioned him, "that they might cross him, that thereby they might have wherewith to accuse him; but he answered them boldly, and withstood all their questions, yea, to their astonishment" (Mosiah 12:19). Then Abinadi asked them a question, "What teach ye this people? And they said: We teach the law of Moses. And again he said unto them: If ye teach the law of Moses why do ye not keep it? Why do ye set your hearts upon riches? Why do ye commit whoredoms and spend your strength with harlots, yea, and cause this people to commit sin . . . ?" (Mosiah 12:27–29).

When the wicked priests claimed that salvation came by the law of Moses, Abinadi testified that it was necessary to keep the commandments of God to be saved. He began quoting the Ten Commandments, and accused the priests of disobeying them. King Noah commanded that Abinadi be slain. But when they went to take Abinadi, "he withstood them, and said unto them: Touch me not, for God shall smite you if you lay your hands upon me, for I have not delivered the message which the Lord sent me to deliver. . . . Now it came to pass . . . that the people of king Noah durst not lay their hands on him, for the

Spirit of the Lord was upon him; and his face shone with exceeding luster, even as Moses' did while in the mount of Sinai, while speaking with the Lord" (Mosiah 13:2–3, 5).

Abinadi finished teaching the Ten Commandments and explained "that salvation doth not come by the law alone; and were it not for the atonement, which God himself shall make for the sins and iniquities of his people, that they must unavoidably perish, notwithstanding the law of Moses" (Mosiah 13:28).

Alma believed Abinadi's teachings, "therefore he began to plead with the king that he would not be angry with Abinadi, but suffer that he might depart in peace" (Mosiah 17:2). But king Noah was angry and commanded that Alma be "cast out from among them, and sent his servants after him that they might slay him" (Mosiah 17:3). However, Alma escaped and went into hiding where he recorded Abinadi's teachings. Alma repented of his sins, and "went about privately among the people, and began to teach the words of Abinadi" (Mosiah 18:1). About two hundred people gathered to hear Alma. They desired to repent and be baptized (see Mosiah 18:1–15).

Alma's followers later escaped to the land of Zarahemla (see Mosiah 23–24). Because of Alma's repentance and desire to serve God, "king Mosiah granted unto Alma that he might establish churches throughout all the land of Zarahemla; and gave him power to ordain priests and teachers over every church" (Mosiah 25:19).

ALMA THE YOUNGER

Alma's son, Alma the Younger, was "a very wicked and an idolatrous man" (Mosiah 27:8). He, with the four sons of king Mosiah, went about "seeking to destroy the church, and to lead astray the people of the Lord" (Mosiah 27:10). "As they were going about rebelling against God, behold, the angel of the Lord appeared unto them; and he descended as it were in a cloud; and he spake as it were with a voice of thunder, which caused the earth to shake" (Mosiah 27:11). Alma and the four sons of Mosiah fell to the earth, "for great was their astonishment; for with their own eyes they had beheld an angel of the Lord; and his voice was as thunder, which shook the earth; and they knew that there was nothing save the power of God that could shake the earth and cause it to tremble as though it would part asunder. And now the astonishment of Alma was so great that he became dumb, that he could not open his mouth; yea, and he became weak, even that he could not move his hands; therefore . . . he was laid before his father" (Mosiah 27:18–19).

Alma's father gathered the priests and they began to fast and pray that Alma might receive his strength and be able to speak. After two days and nights, Alma's strength returned, and he bore a powerful testimony of the redeeming power of the Savior: "I have repented of my sins, and have been redeemed of the Lord; behold I am born of the Spirit."

Alma continued his testimony declaring that,

> All mankind . . . must be born again; yea, born of God, changed from their carnal and fallen state, to a state of righteousness . . . and unless they do this, they can in nowise inherit the kingdom of God. I say unto you, unless this be the case, they must be cast off; and this I know, because I was like to be cast off. Nevertheless, after wading through much tribulation, repenting nigh unto death, the Lord in mercy hath seen fit to snatch me out of an everlasting burning, and I am born of God. My soul hath been redeemed from the gall of bitterness and bonds of

iniquity. I was in the darkest abyss; but now I behold the marvelous light of God. My soul was racked with eternal torment; but I am snatched, my soul is pained no more. (Mosiah 27:24–29)

Years later, Alma related this incredible experience to his son, Helaman. Alma's beautiful testimony is recorded in Alma 36.

After fourteen years of serving as high priest over the Church, Alma expressed his desire to help bring people to Christ:

> **O that I were an angel, and could have the wish of mine heart, that I might go forth and speak with the trump of God, with a voice to shake the earth, and cry repentance unto every people! Yea, I would declare unto every soul, as with the voice of thunder, repentance and the plan of redemption, that they should repent and come unto our God, that there might not be more sorrow upon all the face of the earth. . . . And this is my glory, that perhaps I may be an instrument in the hands of God to bring some soul to repentance; and this is my joy.** (Alma 29:1–2, 9)

THE FOUR SONS OF KING MOSIAH

Shortly after the startling visit of the angel, the four sons of king Mosiah requested permission from their father to go to the land of Nephi as missionaries to the Lamanites **"for they could not bear that any human soul should perish"** (Mosiah 28:3). Their miraculous fourteen-year mission is recorded in Alma, chapters 17 to 26. They brought thousands to the knowledge of the gospel, to baptism and to receive forgiveness for their sins by having faith in the Savior unto repentance. (See Alma 19:33, 36; 24:10–11; 26:1, 3–9, 12–15.)

At the end of their mission Ammon rejoiced because of their incredible successes:

> My brothers and my brethren, behold I say unto you, how great reason have we to rejoice; for could we have supposed when we started from the land of Zarahemla that God would have granted unto us such great blessings? ... Our brethren, the Lamanites, were in darkness ... but behold, how many of them are brought to behold the marvelous light of God! ... We have been made instruments in the hands of God to bring about this great work. (Alma 26:1, 3)

> Let us glory, yea, we will glory in the Lord; yea, we will rejoice, for our joy is full; yea, we will praise our God forever. Behold, who can glory too much in the Lord? Yea, who can say too much of his great power, and of his mercy, and of his long-suffering towards the children of men? Behold, I say unto you, I cannot say the smallest part which I feel. Who could have supposed that our God would have been so merciful as to have snatched us from our awful, sinful, and polluted state? Behold we went forth even in wrath, with mighty threatenings to destroy his church. Oh then, why did he not consign us to an awful destruction, yea, why did he not let the sword of his justice fall upon us, and doom us to eternal despair? Oh, my soul, almost as it were, fleeth at the thought. Behold, he did not exercise his justice upon us, but in his great mercy hath brought us over that everlasting gulf of death and misery, even to the salvation of our souls. (Alma 26:16–20; see also verses 21–34)

Then, Ammon concludes with this exultation:

> Now have we not reason to rejoice? Yea, I say unto you, there never were men that had so great reason to rejoice as we, since the world began; yea, and my joy

is carried away, even unto boasting in my God; for he
has all power, all wisdom, and all understanding; he
comprehendeth all things, and he is a merciful Being,
even unto salvation, to those who repent and believe
on his name . . . this is my life and my light, my joy
and my salvation, and my redemption from everlasting wo. (Alma 26:35–36)

KING LAMONI'S FATHER

While on his mission among the Lamanites, Aaron,
one of king Mosiah's sons, was led by the Spirit to visit
the Lamanite king over all the land, who was the father of
king Lamoni. Aaron answered the old king's questions and
taught him the plan of redemption including the Atonement
of Jesus Christ. After learning about eternal life, Lamoni's
father asked Aaron, **"What shall I do that I may have this
eternal life of which thou hast spoken? Yea, what shall I
do that I may be born of God, having this wicked spirit
rooted out of my breast, and receive his Spirit, that I may
be filled with joy, that I may not be cast off at the last
day?"** (Alma 22:15).

Aaron said to him, **"If thou wilt bow down before
God, yea, if thou wilt repent of all thy sins, . . . and call
on his name in faith, believing that ye shall receive, then
shalt thou receive the hope which thou desirest"** (Alma
22:16).

Obediently, the old king knelt down upon his knees
and prayed: **"O God, Aaron hath told me that there is
a God; and if there is a God, and if thou art God, wilt
thou make thyself known unto me, and I will give away
all my sins to know thee, and that I may be raised from
the dead, and be saved at the last day"** (Alma 22:18). The
king was overpowered by the Spirit, and was converted to

the Lord. He sent a proclamation forbidding his people to harm Ammon and his brethren and granting them free access to the people's houses, temples, and sanctuaries, "**that the word of God might have no obstruction . . . and thus they began to have great success. And thousands were brought to the knowledge of the Lord**" (Alma 23:3–5).

ZEEZROM

Alma the Younger, the high priest over the church, and his companion, Amulek, preached repentance to the wicked people of the city of Ammonihah. Zeezrom, one of the lawyers of the city, "**did stir up the people to riotings, and all manner of disturbances and wickedness, that they might have more employ . . . [and] was expert in the devices of the devil, that he might destroy that which was good**" (Alma 11:20–21). By devious questioning, Zeezrom tried to make it appear that Amulek had contradicted himself (Alma 11:21–35). Amulek called Zeezrom a liar: "**Behold thou hast lied**" (Alma 11:36).

Under the inspiration of the Spirit, Amulek taught Zeezrom, and the people nearby who were listening, true doctrine regarding the resurrection and final judgment (Alma 11:36–45). Zeezrom was astonished for he knew that he had lied and feared to face the final judgment of God. He began to tremble. Seeing the effect of Amulek's teachings on Zeezrom, Alma began to "**establish the words of Amulek, and to explain things beyond, or to unfold the scriptures beyond that which Amulek had done**" (Alma 12:1), telling him that he had not only lied to men, "**but thou hast lied unto God; for behold, he knows all thy thoughts**" (Alma 12:3). Alma explained that Zeezrom had been deceived into lying so that the devil might gain power over him, as well as the people of Ammonihah. Zeezrom felt guilty because "**he**

was convinced that they knew the thoughts and intents of his heart" (Alma 12:7). Zeezrom began asking questions about the resurrection and judgment. Alma answered his questions and taught him about the purpose of mortality and the plan of redemption (see Alma 12:12–37). Many who had been listening believed, but the majority was angry and wanted Alma and Amulek "**put . . . away privily.**" Zeezrom knew he had lied, and so he defended Alma and Amulek, saying, "**I am guilty, and these men are spotless before God**" (Alma 14:3, 7). The people reviled Zeezrom and cast him out of their city. Zeezrom fled to the city of Sidom, gravely concerned about Alma and Amulek.

After completing their mission, Alma and Amulek also went to Sidom. Zeezrom requested that they come to him,

> **And they found him upon his bed, sick, being very low with a burning fever; and his mind also was exceedingly sore because of his iniquities; and when he saw them he stretched forth his hand, and besought them that they would heal him. And it came to pass that Alma said unto him, taking him by the hand: Believest thou in the power of Christ unto salvation? And he answered and said: Yea, I believe all the words that thou hast taught. And Alma said: If thou believest in the redemption of Christ thou canst be healed.** (Alma 15:5–8)

Because of his exceeding faith, Zeezrom was miraculously healed (see Alma 15:9–11). "**And Alma baptized Zeezrom unto the Lord; and he began from that time forth to preach unto the people**" (Alma 15:12).

In addition to these accounts of individuals who repented and obtained forgiveness and atonement for their sins, the Book of Mormon contains a beautiful discourse regarding the Atonement given by the resurrected Savior

Himself during His three-day ministry in America (see 3 Nephi 27:13–21). To have the resurrected Redeemer's actual words testifying of his infinite Atonement is one of the great blessings of the Book of Mormon.

> **I came into the world to do the will of my Father, because my Father sent me. And my Father sent me that I might be lifted up upon the cross . . . that I might draw all men unto me . . . therefore, according to the power of the Father I will draw all men unto me, that they may be judged according to their works . . . Repent . . . and come unto me and be baptized in my name, that ye may be sanctified by the reception of the Holy Ghost, that ye may stand spotless before me at the last day.** (3 Nephi 27:13–15, 20)

The message of the Book of Mormon is that *everyone who comes to the Savior and truly repents will find mercy and be forgiven and will be saved in the Kingdom of God.*

Notes

1. Joseph Fielding Smith, *Answers to Gospel Questions* (Salt Lake City: Deseret Book, 1980), 4:57.
2. Jeffrey R. Holland, *Christ and the New Covenant: The Messianic Message of the Book of Mormon* (Salt Lake City: Deseret Book, 1997), 3–4.

4

CLASSIC DOCTRINAL DISCOURSES AND REVELATIONS

I have selected a few discourses from the Book of Mormon which I consider to be wonderful, masterful works of inspired revelation. I do not believe a mere mortal could have written any of them without divine inspiration. I encourage you to prayerfully read and study any or all of these discourses. My explanations may help your understanding, but I believe that the full benefit can only be realized by those who prayerfully study these discourses with sincere desire to know truth. In my opinion, anyone who believes that Joseph Smith wrote any of these revelations on his own must also believe that he was one of the greatest prophets of all time.

LEHI'S VISION OF THE TREE OF LIFE

This first discourse, found in 1 Nephi 8, comes from a dream or vision Lehi had while camped in the wilderness. **"I beheld a tree, whose fruit was desirable to make one happy . . . I did go forth and partake of the fruit thereof; and I beheld that it was most sweet, above all that I ever before tasted. Yea, and I beheld that the fruit thereof was**

white, to exceed all the whiteness that I had ever seen. And as I partook of the fruit thereof it filled my soul with exceedingly great joy" (1 Nephi 8:10–12). Imagine what an incredible experience it would be to actually taste of this fruit! Re-read the above paragraph paying particular attention to the characteristics of the fruit.

Lehi also saw a "**river of water . . .**" and

> **a rod of iron, and it extended along the bank of the river, and led to the tree by which I stood. And I also beheld a strait and narrow path, which came along by the rod of iron . . . And it came to pass that there arose a mist of darkness . . . insomuch that they who had commenced in the path did lose their way, that they wandered off and were lost.**
>
> **And it came to pass that I beheld others pressing forward, and they came forth and caught hold of the end of the rod of iron; and they did press forward through the mist of darkness, clinging to the rod of iron, even until they did come forth and partake of the fruit of the tree. And after they had partaken of the fruit of the tree they did cast their eyes about as if they were ashamed.**

Lehi also saw "**on the other side of the river of water, a great and spacious building; and it stood as it were in the air, . . . and it was filled with people, both old and young, both male and female; and their manner of dress was exceedingly fine; and they were in the attitude of mocking and pointing their fingers towards those who had come at and were partaking of the fruit,**" which caused some to become "**ashamed, . . . and they fell away into forbidden paths and were lost.**" Lehi saw other groups of people, some trying to find the path, some trying to get to the building, and others wandering lost (1 Nephi 8:13, 19-20, 23–28).

Elder Boyd K. Packer asked some thought provoking questions about Lehi's vision: "Who wrote this incredible vision? There is nothing like it in the Bible. Did Joseph Smith compose it? Did he write the Book of Mormon? That is harder to believe than the account of angels and golden plates. Joseph Smith was only 24 years old when the Book of Mormon was published."[1]

Nephi prayed to know the interpretation of his father's dream and was given a remarkable vision of Christ. Nephi saw,

> **A virgin, most beautiful and fair above all other virgins . . . And it came to pass that I beheld that she was carried away in the Spirit; and after she had been carried away in the Spirit for the space of a time the angel spake unto me, saying: Look! And I looked and beheld the virgin again, bearing a child in her arms. And the angel said unto me: Behold the Lamb of God, yea, even the Son of the Eternal Father!** (1 Nephi 11:15, 19–21).

Then, the angel asked Nephi, "**Knowest thou the meaning of the tree which thy father saw? And I answered him, saying: Yea, it is the love of God . . . wherefore, it is the most desirable above all things. . . . Yea, and the most joyous to the soul**" (1 Nephi 11:21–23). This is the same message found in John 3:16: "For God so loved the world, that he gave his only begotten Son, that whosoever believeth in him should not perish, but have everlasting life." Lehi's dream is a beautiful expression of Heavenly Father's love for us in sending his Son to be our Redeemer, and of the Savior's love for his willingness to do his Father's will by suffering and dying for us that we might be resurrected and obtain forgiveness for our sins.

Elder Boyd K. Packer said, "That vision (Lehi's dream)

is the central message of the Book of Mormon."[2] The Savior's birth, life, mission, atoning sacrifice, and teachings are taught repeatedly throughout the Book of Mormon. The pure gospel of Jesus Christ is the only path that leads to the tree of life—the only source of true, eternal happiness and joy.

Your life, as well as the lives of all mortals, is portrayed in Lehi's dream. Because of the Atonement of Jesus Christ, the way or path has been prepared for you to reach the tree of eternal life and find eternal happiness and joy. But along the way you will encounter temptation, the "**mist of darkness,**" to disobey God's commandments. There are enticing side trips to lead you astray. However, if you will accept baptism and receive the gift of the Holy Ghost, and then hold "**fast to the rod of iron**"—the "**word of God**"—you will be able to arrive at the tree of life and partake of its fruit. However, even "**after**" tasting of the fruit of the tree of life, there will be people mocking you as you try to live the gospel. You must be able to endure "**scoffing**" and not become "**ashamed.**" You must ignore those who make fun of you for being a true Christian. "**For as many as heeded them, had fallen away**" (1 Nephi 8:28–34). (See 1 Nephi 11:14–36 for a more complete interpretation of Lehi's dream.)

FREEDOM OF CHOICE

The second discourse, found in 2 Nephi 2, deals with one of God's greatest gifts to his children, the gift of agency, or the freedom to choose. This Book of Mormon chapter is unique because it goes against the teachings of all the so-called Christian religions that denigrate Adam for partaking of the forbidden fruit. The truth is that: *The Fall of Adam and Eve was part of our Heavenly Father's plan from the beginning!* The Fall made mortality possible, so we could each obtain a physical body, be tested, and then, have the opportunity through the Atonement of Jesus Christ to obtain eternal life, *the greatest of all the gifts of God!* (D&C 14:7). As you consider the teachings in 2 Nephi 2, ask yourself: Do you really think young Joseph Smith or any of his associates could be its author?

The aged prophet Lehi spoke to his son Jacob, who as a child had "**suffered afflictions and much sorrow, because of the rudeness of thy brethren**" (verse 1). Lehi assured Jacob that God "**shall consecrate thine afflictions for thy gain**" (verse 2). What a comforting message for all those who have suffered abuse!

Each of us is an agent unto ourself (free to act for ourself). We have the laws or commandments of God and the freedom to obey or disobey. However, once we choose, we will receive the consequence that is affixed to our choice: happiness if we obey, punishment if we disobey. In other words we have the freedom to choose between good and evil, but once we choose, we will receive the direct consequences of our choice.

Lehi explained that to have agency, "**it must needs be, that there is an opposition in all things**" (verse 11). In other words, in order to have choices there must be opposites: good and evil, sweet and bitter, hot and cold. For this reason, it was necessary for Adam and Eve to partake of the fruit of the tree of knowledge of good and evil. They and we need this knowledge to be able to use our agency to choose good.

Because of the Fall, each of us inherits the right to choose for ourselves—the precious gift of agency. From the beginning, Heavenly Father had the Plan of Redemption all in place. After the creation, Adam and Eve were placed in the Garden of Eden. By choosing to partake of the fruit of the tree of knowledge of good and evil, Adam and Eve made it possible for mankind to be born into this world where we would obtain physical bodies, experience mortality, and have the opportunity to develop a god-like character. The loving Savior would fulfill his Father's plan by coming to redeem mankind from the Fall.

> **All things have been done in the wisdom of him who knoweth all things. Adam fell that men might be; and men are, that they might have joy. And the Messiah cometh in the fulness of time, that he may redeem the children of men from the fall. And because that they are redeemed from the fall they have become free forever, knowing good from evil; to act for themselves and not to be acted upon, save it be by the punishment of the law at the great and last day, according to the commandments which God hath given. Wherefore, men are free according to the flesh; and all things are given them which are expedient unto man. And they are free to choose liberty and eternal life, through the great Mediator of all men, or to choose captivity and death, according to the captivity and power of the devil; for he seeketh that all men might be miserable like unto himself.** (verses 24–27)

For a wonderful explanation of how the Atonement rescues mankind from the Fall, see Samuel the Lamanite's call to repentance in Helaman 14:11–19.

COMPARISON OF THE WORD OF GOD UNTO A SEED

This discourse by the prophet Alma gives us a powerful analogy about the development of faith. It compares the growth of a seed to how the word of God will swell within the heart of an honest inquirer. This analogy is beautifully explained in Alma 32:28–43. I strongly suggest that you *prayerfully read* these verses several times.

How do you plant the word in your heart? What is the word? Alma was asked this question and his answer is recorded in Alma 33:22. Planting the word means that you

- Believe in the Son of God.
- Believe that He came to redeem all mankind.
- Believe that He suffered and died to atone for your sins.
- Believe that He was resurrected.
- Believe that you will stand before Him at the judgment day to be judged for your works.

After planting this word (seed) in your heart, you must:

- Give this word (seed) time to germinate and begin to grow within your mind and heart.
- Pray and ask God if Jesus Christ is the Redeemer of mankind.
- Study the scriptures about the life and mission of the Savior.
- Do your best to live a Christlike life.
- Keep the Sabbath day holy.
- Continue to nourish the word (seed) with faith, diligence, and patience.

Will you have faith to plant the word (seed) in your heart? Only you can answer this vital question. If *you have sufficient faith* to try this exciting experiment there are two possible results:

1. *It will grow* if you do not cast it out by your unbelief. It will begin as a tiny seedling.

This seedling *must* be constantly nourished or it will die. If you sincerely pray and study the word and live the best you can, you will begin to feel swelling emotions within your breast.

These feelings will be real and exciting. The sprout will grow slowly, but steadily, as long as you nourish it daily.

If you continue faithful, it will become a young tree.

With time and constant nourishment and care the young tree will eventually become a mature tree bearing the fruit of everlasting life.

You will receive true joy and eternal happiness! (See Alma 32:41–43)

2. *Or it will die*—if you neglect the word (sprout), it will shrivel up and die, because it cannot continue to live and grow unless it receives daily nourishment through your earnest prayer, study, and obedience (see Alma 32:40).

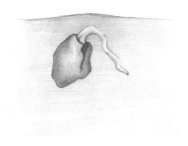

Even though the word (seed) is true (good), it will not get root in you and begin to grow unless *you do your part.* Heavenly Father and the Savior have done all they can. *Now, the rest is up to you!!* Pray for help in knowing and understanding the truth, and begin reading the Book of Mormon. An excellent place to begin is 1 Nephi chapter one. If you exercise your faith, an exciting experience with the word of God awaits you: **"It will begin to swell within your breasts; and when you feel these swelling motions, ye will begin to say within yourselves—It must needs be that this is a good seed, or that the word is good, for it beginneth to enlarge my soul; yea, it beginneth to enlighten my understanding, yea, it beginneth to be delicious to me"** (Alma 32:28).

When this marvelous experience happens to you, you have received revelation from the Holy Ghost. You have received a testimony that *the Book of Mormon is true!*

THE LAWS OF JUSTICE AND MERCY

This lofty dissertation, found in Alma 42, also comes from Alma the younger. He had a wayward son, Corianton, who left his mission to go after the harlot, Isabel. In Alma 39–42, Alma taught his son why he needed to repent of this extremely serious sin. Alma answered Corianton's question regarding **"the justice of God in the punishment of the sinner; for** (Alma explained) **ye do try to suppose that it is injustice that the sinner should be consigned to a state of misery"** (Alma 42:1). Even today, some may wonder if sinners will be punished. Alma explained that according to **"the great plan of happiness,"** (Alma 42:8) after the Fall of Adam and Eve, mankind was placed in a probationary or preparatory state, and if there were no redemption, mankind would be miserable forever **"being cut off from the** presence of the Lord ... because of his own disobedience" (Alma 42:11–12).

MY SINS

The eternal law of justice affixes a punishment to every sin. Alma explained that "**God would cease to be God**" if he were to allow unrepentant sinners to go unpunished letting "**mercy . . . rob justice**" (Alma 42:13, 25). Alma explained how God's great plan of redemption and happiness satisfies the law of justice through the Atonement and brings about the plan of mercy. The plan of mercy could only be brought about through an atonement by a God who would suffer for the sins of the world (Alma 42:14–15). On conditions of repentance, we can obtain forgiveness because God's suffering will replace our suffering; otherwise, we must suffer for our own sins. Thus, the eternal law of justice can be satisfied by our suffering for our own sins or, if we repent, by the Savior's suffering.

The following visuals illustrate how the Law of Mercy can satisfy the Law of Justice:

THE LAW OF JUSTICE:

If we do not repent, we must suffer for our own sins

THE LAW OF MERCY:

If we repent, Christ offers us mercy by replacing our suffering with His.

Verse 22 summarizes the merciful plan of our Father: **"There is a law given, and a punishment affixed, and a repentance granted; which repentance, mercy claimeth; otherwise, justice claimeth the creature and executeth the law, and the law inflicteth the punishment; if not so, the works of justice would be destroyed, and God would cease to be God. But God ceaseth not to be God, and mercy claimeth the penitent, and mercy cometh because of the atonement"** (Alma 42:22–23). I have studied this chapter and particularly verse 22 for years, and gradually my understanding has grown of this important truth. That's how God's word works. As you study, ponder and pray, and try to be obedient, you learn **"line upon line, precept upon precept, here a little and there a little"** (2 Nephi 28:30). (See also 2 Nephi 28, another wondrous chapter of scripture.)

THE RESURRECTED JESUS CHRIST APPEARS IN AMERICA

The visit of the resurrected Jesus Christ in ancient America, found in 3 Nephi 11, is the crowning event in the Book of Mormon. In AD 34, three hours of devastating earthquakes and tornados left entire cities buried, others burned, and some covered by water. The tempests and terrible destructions were followed by three days of complete darkness

"And it came to pass that there was thick darkness upon all the face of the land, insomuch that the inhabitants . . . could feel the vapor of darkness; and there could be no light, because of the darkness, neither candles, neither torches; neither could there be fire kindled with their fine and exceedingly dry wood, so that there could not be any light at all"

(3 Nephi 8:20–21). Imagine being in total darkness for an extended time!

During the three days of darkness, survivors groaned, wept, and mourned because of the darkness and destruction. The terrible storms had caused widespread devastation. Roads were spoiled, and buildings were damaged. Thousands had been killed. "**The whole face of the land was changed**" (3 Nephi 8:12). All these devastations occurred at the time of the crucifixion of the Savior and were a sign to the inhabitants of the Americas. Those who knew the prophecies of the prophets knew that Jesus Christ had completed the Atonement.

Suddenly a voice was heard by the survivors telling them the extent of the devastation and calling them to repentance:

> **O all ye that are spared because ye were more righteous than they, will ye not now return unto me, and repent of your sins, and be converted, that I may heal you? . . . Behold, I am Jesus Christ the Son of God. . . . Behold, I have come unto the world to bring redemption unto the world, to save the world from sin. Therefore, whoso repenteth and cometh unto me as a little child, him will I receive, for of such is the kingdom of God.** (3 Nephi 9:13, 15, 21–22)

The voice ceased speaking. Silence prevailed for many hours. Then, once again, the voice was heard throughout the land, pleading with the people to repent and promising to gather them. The darkness was disbursed, and although the people lamented the loss of their loved ones, "**their mourning was turned into joy, and their lamentations into the praise and thanksgiving unto the Lord Jesus Christ, their Redeemer**" (3 Nephi 10:10).

Soon after the Savior's ascension into heaven in Jerusalem, a group of Nephites had gathered at the temple in the land Bountiful on the American continent. They heard a voice from heaven, and although it was "**a small voice it did pierce them that did hear to the center**" (3 Nephi 11:3). The third time they heard the voice they understood and looked heavenward from whence the voice came.

The voice said to them,

> **Behold my Beloved Son, in whom I am well pleased, in whom I have glorified my name—hear ye him. . . . [T]hey saw a Man descending out of heaven; and he was clothed in a white robe. . . . And it came to pass that he stretched forth his hand and spake unto the people, saying: Behold, I am Jesus Christ, whom the prophets testified shall come into the world. And behold, I am the light and the life of the world; I have drunk out of that bitter cup which the Father hath given me, and have glorified the Father in taking upon me the sins of the world.** (3 Nephi 11:7–11)

The multitude fell to the earth, and Jesus said unto them:

> **Arise and come forth unto me, that ye may thrust your hands into my side, and also that ye may feel the prints of the nails in my hands and in my feet, that ye may know that I am the God of Israel, and the God of the whole earth, and have been slain for the sins of the world. And it came to pass that the multitude went forth, and thrust their hands into his side, and did feel the prints of the nails in his hands and in his feet; and this they did do, going forth one by one until they had all gone forth, and did see with their eyes and did feel with their hands, and did know of a surety and did bear record, that it was he, of whom it was written by the prophets, that should come.** (3 Nephi 11:14–15)

After the multitude had witnessed of him, they cried out: "**Hosanna! Blessed be the name of the Most High**

God! And they did fall down at the feet of Jesus, and did worship him" (3 Nephi 11:17). Jesus continued to minister for three days among the people. The Savior called twelve disciples and gave them authority to baptize. He organized His church as He had done in Jerusalem. He gave them specific instructions on how they were to baptize:

> **"On this wise shall ye baptize; and there shall be no disputations among you. Verily I say unto you, that whoso repenteth of his sins through your words, and desireth to be baptized in my name, on this wise shall ye baptize them—Behold, ye shall go down and stand in the water, and in my name shall ye baptize them. And now behold, these are the words which ye shall say . . . Having authority given me of Jesus Christ, I baptize you in the name of the Father, and of the Son, and of the Holy Ghost. Amen. And then shall ye immerse them in the water, and come forth again out of the water.** (3 Nephi 11:22–26)

The Savior taught the people His doctrine (see 3 Nephi 11:28–41) and delivered a discourse similar to the Sermon on the Mount, which He had delivered near the Sea of Galilee. (Carefully compare 3 Nephi 12–14 with Matthew 5–7.)

After teaching the people that the law of Moses had been fulfilled and that they should no more offer blood sacrifices, Jesus said: **"Behold, I am the law, and the light. Look unto me, and endure unto the end, and ye shall live; for unto him that endureth to the end will I give eternal life"** (3 Nephi 15:9). Jesus taught and ministered among the people, healing their lame, their blind, their halt, their maimed, their leprous, their withered, their deaf, and all who had any kind of affliction. He blessed their little children and had the multitude kneel as he knelt and prayed for them.

The record-keeper recorded:

The eye hath never seen, neither hath the ear heard, before, so great and marvelous things as we saw and heard Jesus speak unto the Father; and no tongue can speak, neither can there be written by any man, neither can the hearts of men conceive so great and marvelous things as we both saw and heard Jesus speak; and no one can conceive of the joy which filled our souls at the time we heard him pray for us unto the Father.

And it came to pass that when Jesus had made an end of praying unto the Father, he arose; but so great was the joy of the multitude that they were overcome. And it came to pass that Jesus spake unto them and bade them arise. And they arose from the earth, and he said unto them: Blessed are ye because of your faith. And now behold, my joy is full. And when he had said these words, he wept, and the multitude bare record of it, and he took their little children, one by one, and blessed them, and prayed unto the Father for them. And when he had done this he wept again. (3 Nephi 17:16–22)

Jesus instituted the ordinance of the sacrament among the Nephites (see 3 Nephi 18:1–12) and instructed them to "**Watch and pray always, lest ye be tempted by the devil, and ye be led away captive by him. . . . Behold, verily, verily, I say unto you, ye must watch and pray always lest ye enter into temptation; for Satan desireth to have you, that he may sift you as wheat**" (3 Nephi 18:15, 18).

The prophet Mormon who abridged the original records wrote concerning the words of Christ, "**And wo be unto him that will not hearken unto the words of Jesus, and also to them whom he hath chosen and sent among them; for whoso receiveth not the words of Jesus and the words of those whom he hath sent receiveth not him; and therefore he will not receive them at the last day**" (3 Nephi 28:34). Thus, began an unprecedented period of nearly two hundred years of millennial-like peace (see 4 Nephi 1:1–18, 23–24).

For the complete account of the Savior's visit to the Americas see 3 Nephi 9–28.

THE DOCTRINE OR GOSPEL OF CHRIST

The doctrine or gospel of Jesus Christ is taught throughout the Book of Mormon, but is explained in great detail in Second and Third Nephi. We are taught why living this doctrine is the only way whereby man can qualify for the full blessings of the Atonement. A study of this doctrine reveals the following major points:

1. The Father, Son, and Holy Ghost bear record of each other.
2. Jesus Christ is the Lamb of God who came into the world to do the will of the Father.
3. Jesus Christ suffered in Gethsemane and was crucified for the sins of all mankind.
4. Because of the Savior's resurrection, every person born into mortality will be resurrected.
5. All mankind will stand before the Savior to be judged according to their works.
6. All who repent, are baptized, receive the Holy Ghost, and endure to the end shall be held guiltless before the Father at the Day of Judgment.

No unclean thing can enter into his kingdom; therefore nothing entereth into his rest save it be those who have washed their garments in my blood, because of their faith, and the repentance of all their sins, and their faithfulness unto the end. Now this is the commandment: Repent, all ye ends of the earth, and come unto me and be baptized in my name, that ye may be sanctified by the reception of the Holy

Ghost, that ye may stand spotless before me at the last day. (3 Nephi 27:19–20)

The doctrine or gospel of Christ is simple and is put forth in the following references so clearly that even a child can understand it:

- 2 Nephi 31:2–21; 32:1–6
- 3 Nephi 11:32–41
- 3 Nephi 27:13–22

FAITH, HOPE, AND CHARITY

In Moroni 7, Moroni writes "**a few of the words of my father Mormon, which he spake concerning faith, hope, and charity**" (Moroni 7:1). This inspired discourse answers several profound questions such as:

- Why *must* we pray with "**real intent of heart?** What is the significance of the words, "**it profiteth him nothing** (See Moroni 7:6–9)
- Why can't an evil man do that which is good? (See Moroni 7:10–11)
- How would you define "good"? How does the Lord define "good"? How can we discern good from evil? What spiritual gift "**is given to every man**"? (See Moroni 7:12–24)
- How can we obtain all which is good? What can be obtained through faith? (See Moroni 7:25–39)

Mormon said,

> **And as surely as Christ liveth he spake these words . . . saying: Whatsoever thing ye shall ask the Father in my name, which is good, in faith believing that ye shall receive, behold, it shall be done unto you. . . . If ye will have faith in me ye shall have power**

**to do whatsoever thing is expedient in me. . . . Repent
all ye ends of the earth, and come unto me, and be
baptized in my name, and have faith in me, that ye
may be saved.** (Moroni 7:26, 33, 34)

- Since God is the same yesterday, today, and forever,
  what would be the reason miracles are not occurring
  among a people? What does God provide to help us
  have faith in him? What is required of us in order to
  be saved? (See Moroni 7:27–38)
- How does one obtain hope? (See Moroni 7:40–43)
- What is charity, and how is it attained? What are
  the character traits of a truly charitable person? (See
  Moroni 7:44–48)

While abridging the twenty-four Plates of Ether, Moroni
added his own commentary about faith (see Ether 12:6–
41). He defines faith as follow: "**Faith is things which are
hoped for and not seen; wherefore, dispute not because
ye see not, for ye receive no witness until after the trial
of your faith**" (Ether 12:6). Moroni then listed several
examples miracles wrought by faith from scripture (see Ether
12:10–21). Read about the miracle that can occur in your
life in Ether 12:27.

INFANT BAPTISM IS
AN EVIL ABOMINATION

Moroni 8 is a letter written to Moroni by his father,
Mormon. Mormon was "**exceedingly**" grieved to learn of
"**disputations among you concerning the baptism of
your little children.**" Mormon asked Moroni to "**labor
diligently, that this gross error should be removed from
among you.**" Mormon explained that "**little children are**

whole, for they are not capable of committing sin . . . it is solemn mockery before God, that ye should baptize little children" (Moroni 8:5–6, 8–9).

Mormon further explained that "little children need no repentance, neither baptism. Behold, baptism is unto repentance to the fulfilling the commandments unto the remission of sins. But little children are alive in Christ . . . if not so, God is a partial God . . . for how many little children have died without baptism! . . . For awful is the wickedness to suppose that God saveth one child because of baptism, and the other must perish because he hath no baptism" (Moroni 8:11–12, 15).

Notes

1. Boyd K. Packer, "Finding Ourselves in Lehi's Dream," *Ensign*, Aug. 2010, 23.
2. Boyd K. Packer, "The Things of My Soul," *Ensign*, May 1986, 59.

5

THE INSPIRING EFFECT OF
REPEATED READINGS

Most readers read a book only once, especially if it is fiction. Occasionally readers may read the same book a second or third time, but for a book to be read over and over is rare. Members of The Church of Jesus Christ of Latter-day Saints are encouraged by their leaders to read daily from the Book of Mormon throughout their lives. As stated in the Foreword, I have read the Book of Mormon fifty to sixty times. It continues to be my absolute favorite book. I look forward to reading at least one chapter first thing each morning.

For years, I have wondered what it is about the Book of Mormon that makes reading, studying, and pondering its passages so stimulating. There is a power in the word of the Lord that we do not find in other writings. I have come to feel much like Nephi expressed: "**For my soul delighteth in the scriptures, and my heart pondereth them** (2 Nephi 4:15).

The more familiar I become with the text, the more I see real life applications. I am amazed that no matter how many times I read the chapters in sequence, the particular chapter I am reading that day applies perfectly to something that is happening in my life at that time. I especially love the doctrinal chapters, and sometimes read them two or three days in a row. I do not read fast because each word is often significant.

I have a special red pencil that I "must" have when I read because I find words or phrases that I want to mark, even though I'm reading a previously marked chapter. Sometimes I underline and other times I color whole words or phrases. Often, I write cross-references in the margins when another passage adds to the meaning of a particular verse.

Following are examples of inspirational passages I have marked:

1 Nephi 10:19–22	Alma 5:14–19	Alma 34:17–27
2 Nephi 2:24–27	Alma 5:45–48	Alma 34:30–34
2 Nephi 4:15–18	Alma 5:53–56	Alma 34:39–41
2 Nephi 9:10–15	Alma 5:57–58	Alma 37: 9–10
2 Nephi 25:17–19	Alma 7:14–16	Alma 37:33–37
2 Nephi 28:29–30	Alma 12:13–15	Alma 37:38–47
Jacob 6:5–8	Alma 13:27–29	Alma 39:7–15
Jacob 7:12	Alma 22:15–16	Alma 40:11–14
Enos 1:26–27	Alma 24:8–10	Alma 41:3–7
Omni 1:26	Alma 30:43–44	Alma 41:10–15
Mosiah 2:22–24,	Alma 31:5–11	Alma 42:1–26
41	Alma 31:24–28	Alma 42:27–30
Mosiah 3:17,19	Alma 32:1–6	Alma 43:43–47
Mosiah 5:7–15	Alma 32:12–16	Alma 46:23–26
Mosiah 18:8–10	Alma 33:2–9	Alma 48:1–3
Mosiah 26:15–24	Alma 33:19–23	Alma 48:7–10
Mosiah 27:24–26	Alma 34:4–7	Alma 48:11–18
Alma 5:10–13	Alma 34:8–14	Alma 57:25–27

Alma 62:40–41	3 Nephi 17:5–10	Ether 3:1–20
Alma 62:48–51	3 Nephi 17:15–18	Ether 4:1–7
Helaman 3:27–30	3 Nephi 18:3–13	Ether 4:8–19
Helaman 5:5–12	3 Nephi 18:15–24	Ether 6:2–11
Helaman 10:4–7	3 Nephi 19:26–29	Ether 12:2–31
Helaman 12:7–26	3 Nephi 21:11–22	Ether 12:32–37
Helaman 13:3–5	3 Nephi 23:1–6	Ether 12:38–41
Helaman 13:29,	3 Nephi 27:13–22	Moroni 7:5–34
33, 36, 38	3 Nephi 27:25–29	Moroni 7:35–39
Helaman 14:11–19	Mormon 3:17–22	Moroni 7:40–48
Helaman 14:28–31	Mormon 7:1–5	Moroni 8:5–26
Helaman 15:3	Mormon 7:6–8	Moroni 9:25–26
Helaman 15:7–9	Mormon 9:1–6	Moroni 10:3–5
3 Nephi 9:17–22	Mormon 9:7–21	Moroni 10:6–19
3 Nephi 11:3–11	Mormon 9:22–29	Moroni 10:20–34
3 Nephi 11:12–17	Mormon 9:30–37	
3 Nephi 11:31–39	Ether 2:9–12	

(Sometimes I jokingly say that they ought to print the whole book marked and let us erase those few passages that do not have special meaning.)

The Book of Mormon itself gives great promises to those who diligently read, study, and apply its words in their lives:

"**Whoso would hearken unto the word of God, and would hold fast unto it, they would never perish; neither could the temptations and the fiery darts of the adversary overpower them unto blindness, to lead them away to destruction**" (1 Nephi 15:24).

Speaking of the path that leads to eternal life and exaltation, Nephi tells us to,

"**Press forward with a steadfastness in Christ, having a perfect brightness of hope, and a love of God and of all men. Wherefore, if ye shall press forward, feasting** upon the word of Christ, and endure to the end, behold, thus saith the Father: Ye shall have eternal life" (2 Nephi 31:20). "Feast upon the words of Christ; for behold, the words of Christ will tell you all things what ye should do" (2 Nephi 32:3).

In Alma 37, Alma gives his son, Helaman, charge of the sacred records and instructs him as to why they are so important:

> Keep a record of this people, according as I have done, upon the plates of Nephi, and keep all these things sacred which I have kept, even as I have kept them; for it is for a wise purpose that they are kept . . . they have enlarged the memory of this people, yea, and convinced many of the error of their ways, and brought them to the knowledge of their God unto the salvation of their souls . . . these records and their words brought them unto repentance; that is, they brought them to the knowledge of the Lord their God, and to rejoice in Jesus Christ their Redeemer . . . they are preserved for a wise purpose . . . that he may show forth his power unto future generations. . . .
>
> And now, my son, I have somewhat to say concerning the thing which our fathers call a ball, or director—or our fathers called it Liahona, which is, being interpreted, a compass; and the Lord prepared it. (Alma 37:2, 8–9, 12, 14, 38)

The Lord prepared the Liahona to guide Lehi and his family as they journeyed into the wilderness in obedience to the command to leave Jerusalem. It was "a round ball of curious workmanship; and it was of fine brass. And within the ball were two spindles; and the one pointed the way whither we should go" (1 Nephi 16:10).

And it did work for them according to their faith in God; therefore, if they had faith to believe that God could cause that those spindles should point the way they should go, behold, it was done . . . day by day.

Nevertheless, because those miracles were worked by small means it did show unto them marvelous works. They were slothful, and forgot to exercise their faith and diligence and then those marvelous works ceased, and they did not progress in their journey; Therefore, they tarried in the wilderness, or did not travel a direct course, and were afflicted with hunger and thirst, because of their transgressions. (Alma 37:40–42)

Then, Alma applies the principles he has just taught:

And now, my son, [and the following applies to every person who has in his possession a copy of the Book of Mormon] I would that ye should understand that these things are not without a shadow; for as our fathers were slothful to give heed to this compass (now these things were temporal) they did not prosper; even so it is with things that are spiritual. For behold, it is as easy to give heed to the word of Christ, which will point to you a straight course to eternal bliss, as it was for our fathers to give heed to this compass, which would point unto them a straight course to the promised land. And now I say, is there not a type in this thing? For just as surely as this director did bring our fathers, by following its course, to the promised land, shall the words of Christ, if we follow their course, carry us beyond this vale of sorrow into a far better land of promise. (Alma 37:43–45).

In other words, when we have faith to obey its words, the Book of Mormon will guide us in a "direct course" toward the celestial kingdom. The Book of Mormon contains the words of Christ and if we apply them in our lives, they will lead us to greater happiness in this life and to eternal life with our families in the presence of God.

Finally, Alma gives a warning and encouragement: "**Do not let us be slothful because of the easiness of the way; for so was it with our fathers; for so was it prepared for them, that if they would look they might live; even so it is with us. The way is prepared, and if we will look we may live forever . . . see that ye look to God and live**" (Alma 37:46–47).

And so, the Book of Mormon can be one's own personal spiritual compass. If we have faith to look at it daily, to read and ponder its words, and follow its guidance, it will help lead us back to the presence of our Eternal Father to the "**far better land of promise.**"

As we learned in our earlier review of Alma 32, Alma compares

> **the word of God unto a seed. Now, if ye give place, that a seed may be planted in your heart, behold, if it be a true seed, or a good seed, if ye do not cast it out by your unbelief, that ye will resist the Spirit of the Lord, behold, it will begin to swell within your breasts; and when you feel these swelling motions, ye will begin to say within yourselves—It must be that this is a good seed, or that the word is good, for it beginneth to enlarge my soul; yea, it beginneth to enlighten my understanding, yea, it beginneth to be delicious to me.** (Alma 32:28)

This is exactly what happened in my life, and it will happen in anyone's life who plants the true seed (word of God) in his or her heart and diligently gives it nourishment. I love reading from the Book of Mormon, because it is delicious to me and I feel the swelling motions of the truths it contains. (See Comparison of the Word of God unto a Seed on page 43.)

When you come to know by the power of the Holy Ghost that these promises are true it becomes a privilege to read daily from the Book of Mormon. The Book of Mormon is the most profound book I have encountered. It can be read and enjoyed by children who are beginning readers, as well as by scholars who have studied the text for years and have tremendous background in Semitic languages and cultures.

The Book of Mormon may be read and studied at various levels. The first few times I read it, I read mainly to understand the stories and the flow of the history. This may be compared to a swimmer who just barely gets into the water and does not go very deep.

Then, as I continued to read, I began to see applications to my own life. This slowed my reading and helped me see some amazing, beautiful insights I had missed in previous readings. This may be compared to snorkeling and scuba diving. Then, I went much deeper and compared passages throughout the book which interrelate, and I studied cross-references to the Bible and other scriptures. I was in awe of the consistent doctrine and the in-depth teachings that I had never before encountered anywhere.

For an example of the results of a "deep sea diving" approach to scripture study see chapter 9, "God's Own Handwriting." Studying the scriptures in this "deep sea diving" approach must be experienced firsthand to be fully understood and appreciated. It begins with sincere prayer and diligent reading and studying, and is available to everyone.

6

THE PROPHETIC HISTORY OF THE UNITED STATES OF AMERICA

The Prophet Nephi between the years 600 and 592 BC recorded a vision he had of the discovery and colonization of America. Nephi recorded:

> And it came to pass that I looked and beheld many waters [Atlantic Ocean]; and they divided the Gentiles [people of Europe] from the seed of my brethren [Nephi's descendants living in the Americas— Native Americans or Lamanites as referred to in the Book of Mormon].
>
> And it came to pass that the angel said unto me: Behold the wrath [anger] of God is upon the seed of thy brethren.
>
> And I looked and beheld a man among the Gentiles [Columbus], who was separated from the seed of my brethren by the many waters; and I beheld the Spirit of God, that it came down and wrought upon the man [Columbus himself declared: "With a hand that could be felt, the Lord opened my mind to the fact that it would be possible to sail and he opened my will to desire to accomplish the project.... This was the fire that burned within me.... Who can doubt that this fire was not merely mine, but also of the Holy Spirit ... urging

me to press forward"[1]]; **and he went forth upon the many waters, even unto the seed of my brethren, who were in the promised land** [America].

And it came to pass that I beheld the Spirit of God, that it wrought upon other Gentiles [pilgrims and colonizers]; **and they went forth out of captivity, upon the many waters.**

And it came to pass that I beheld many multitudes of the Gentiles [colonists] **upon the land of promise; and I beheld the wrath of God, that it was upon the seed of my brethren; and they were scattered** [driven west] **before the Gentiles and were smitten.**

And I beheld the Spirit of the Lord, that it was upon the Gentiles, and they did prosper and obtain the land for their inheritance; and I beheld that they were white, and exceedingly fair and beautiful, like unto my people before they were slain.

And it came to pass that I, Nephi, beheld that the Gentiles [colonists] **who had gone forth out of captivity did humble themselves before the Lord; and the power of the Lord was with them.**

And I beheld that their mother Gentiles [England and her allies] **were gathered together upon the waters, and upon the land also, to battle** [Revolutionary War] **against them.**

And I beheld that the power of God [providence] **was with them, and also that the wrath of God was upon all those that were gathered together against them to battle.**

And I, Nephi, beheld that the Gentiles [colonists] **that had gone out of captivity were delivered by the power of God out of the hands of all other nations.**

And it came to pass that I, Nephi, beheld that they did prosper in the land; and I beheld a book [Bible], **and it was carried forth among them"** (1 Nephi 13:10–20).

The angel explained that

**there are many plain and precious things taken
away from the book, which is the book of the Lamb
of God. . . . Because of the many plain and precious things which have been taken away out of the
book, . . . an exceedingly great many do stumble**
[there is great confusion among those who believe the
Bible, resulting in hundreds of different interpretations
and denominations]. . . .
**I beheld . . . the book of the Lamb of
God . . . came forth from the Gentiles unto the remnant of the seed of my brethren** [Native Americans/
Lamanites]. **And after it had come forth unto them I
beheld other books** [Book of Mormon], **which came
forth by the power of the Lamb. . . . And the angel
spake unto me saying: These last records** [Book of
Mormon] **. . . shall establish the truth of the first**
[Bible], **. . . and shall make known the plain and precious things . . . that the Lamb of God is the Son of
the Eternal Father, and the Savior of the world; and
that all men must come unto him, or they cannot be
saved** (1 Nephi 13:28–29, 38–40).

Regarding the land of America, the Promised Land, the
Lord declared, "**This is a land which is choice above all
other lands; wherefore he that doth possess it shall serve
God or shall be swept off; for it is the everlasting decree
of God. . . . Behold, this is a choice land and whatsoever
nation shall possess it shall be free from bondage, and
from captivity, and from all other nations under heaven,
if they will but serve the God of the land, who is Jesus
Christ, who hath been manifested by the things which
we have written**" (Ether 2:10, 12).

Note

1. Arnold K. Garr, "Preparing for the Restoration," *Ensign*, June 1999, 34.

7

PLAIN AND PRECIOUS TRUTHS REMOVED FROM THE BIBLE

Hundreds of "Christian" churches claim that the Bible contains all the word of God that we need. They say that the heavens are closed, and there is no need for living prophets or modern revelation. Because of this belief, many claim without even reading the Book of Mormon that it is blasphemy and that Joseph Smith was a fraud. "Perhaps no other book has been denounced so vigorously by those who have never read it as has the Book of Mormon."[1] Those who believe that God's word can only be found in the Bible claim that God has no more to say than what is already in the Bible. They limit His ability to reveal His word today in such trying times or to people anciently who had no access to the Bible. Thus, their belief that God's word can only be found in the Bible has cut them off from receiving more of the word of the Lord.

In about 550 BC, Nephi prophesied that in the latter days, when the Book of Mormon came forth, many would reject it saying: "**A Bible! A Bible! We have got a Bible, and there cannot be any more Bible**" (2 Nephi 29:3). Then, the Lord explains that the Bible came from the Jews and asks if the people have remembered the Jews and thanked them for the Bible. Of course they have not remembered the Jews, nor thanked them for the Bible, but they have hated and cursed them. Then, the Lord asks some provoking questions,

> **Know ye not that there are more nations than one? Know ye not that I, the Lord your God, have created all men, and that I remember those who are upon the isles of the sea; and that I rule in the heavens above and in the earth beneath; and I bring forth my word unto the children of men, yea, even upon all the nations of the earth? Wherefore murmur ye, because that ye shall receive more of my word? Know ye not that the testimony of two nations is a witness unto you that I am God, that I remember one nation like unto another? Wherefore, I speak the same words unto one nation like unto another. And when the two nations shall run together the testimony of the two nations shall run together also. And I do this that I may *prove* unto many that I am the same yesterday, today, and forever . . . and because that I have spoken one word ye need not suppose that I cannot speak another. . . . Wherefore, because that ye have a Bible ye need not suppose that it contains all my words; neither need ye suppose that I have not caused more to be written.** (2 Nephi 29:7–10, italics added).

Those who believe God's word can only be found in the Bible become satisfied and unwilling to receive more of the word of God. In vision, Nephi foresaw the history of America, and he saw the pilgrims coming to America carrying a book. He learned that the book was a record of the Jews that contained many prophecies and covenants of the Lord. This book was the Bible. Nephi saw that when the writings of the apostles first came forth, they "**contained the fulness of the gospel of the Lord,**" but after the apostles were killed and the church fell into apostasy, many plain and precious parts of the gospel were taken out of the Bible causing many to stumble, allowing Satan to have great power over them (see 1 Nephi 13:20–26, 29). **"There are many plain and precious things taken away from the book, which is the book of the Lamb of God. And after these plain and precious things were taken away . . . an exceedingly great many do stumble, yea, insomuch that Satan hath great power over them"** (1 Nephi 13:28–29).

Then, Nephi saw **"other books** (the Book of Mormon, the Doctrine and Covenants, the book of Abraham), **which came forth by the power of the Lamb. . . . These last records . . . shall make known the plain and precious things which have been taken away"** from the Bible (1 Nephi 13:39–40).

The Book of Mormon was prepared by the Lord to come forth in the latter days. How grateful we should be to have more of the word of the Lord, especially to have a record that was translated directly into English by the gift and power of God. The Book of Mormon is truly "plain and precious."

The Lord gives a warning to those who refuse to receive more of his word:

> **Wo be unto him that shall say: We have received the word of God, and we need no more of the word of God, for we have enough! For behold, thus saith the Lord God: I will give unto the children of men line upon line, precept upon precept, here a little and there a little; and blessed are those who hearken unto my precepts, and lend an ear unto my counsel, for they shall learn wisdom; for unto him that receiveth I will give more; and from them that shall say, We have enough, from them shall be taken away even that which they have.** (2 Nephi 28:29–30)

Elder Bruce R. McConkie noted that there is a big

difference between people who believe only the Bible and those who also believe the Book of Mormon. He said: "People who believe the Bible . . . can also believe any creed of their choice and belong to any church that suits them. But belief in the Book of Mormon presupposes the acceptance of Joseph Smith as a prophet as well as membership in the church organized by him. . . .

"Further, the Bible is difficult to interpret and understand, and reasonable men, approaching it wholly from an intellectual standpoint, can reach divergent conclusions on almost all doctrines—hence, the many contending sects in Christendom. The Bible is indeed the perfect tool to support every conceivable doctrinal view. But the Book of Mormon is otherwise; this American scripture sets forth the doctrines of salvation in simplicity and plainness so that reasonable men, even from an intellectual standpoint, can scarcely disagree. This leaves religionists in the position where they must freely accept or openly oppose the Nephite scripture. There is no middle ground, no readily available gray area, no room for compromise."[2]

The doctrine of grace is an example of what happens when men use the Bible alone to determine their beliefs. Some claim that man is saved by grace, not by works. Others teach that one must earn salvation by his righteous works. The Bible appears to be somewhat ambiguous on the doctrine of grace. Consider Acts 15:10–11, which states: "Now therefore why tempt ye God, to put a yoke upon the neck of the disciples, which neither our fathers nor we were able to bear? But we believe that through the grace of the Lord Jesus Christ we shall be saved, even as they."

To further support their belief, they might quote Romans 11:5–6: "Even so then at this present time also there is a remnant according to the election of grace. And if by grace, then is it no more of works: otherwise grace is no more grace. But if it be of works, then is it no more grace: otherwise work is no more work." Another verse they might use to support their belief is Ephesians 2:8–9: "For by grace are ye saved through faith; and that not of yourselves: it is the gift of God: Not of works, lest any man boast."

Those who favor works might point to 1 Peter 1:16–17: "Because it is written, Be ye holy; for I am holy. And if ye call on the Father, who without respect of persons judgeth according to every man's work."

Revelation 22:11–14 states: "He that is unjust, let him be unjust still: and he which is filthy, let him be filthy still: and he that is righteous, let him be righteous still: and he that is holy, let him be holy still. And, behold, I come quickly; and my reward is with me, to give every man according as his work shall be. I am Alpha and Omega, the beginning and the end, the first and the last. Blessed are they that do his commandments, that they may have right to the tree of life, and may enter in through the gates into the city."

Finally, James 2:14, 19–20, 26 declares: "What doth it profit, my brethren, though a man say he hath faith and have not works? can faith save him?. . . Thou believest that there is one God; thou doest well: the devils also believe, and tremble. But wilt thou know, . . . that faith without works is dead? . . . For as the body without the spirit is dead, so faith without works is dead also."

The Book of Mormon comes to our rescue. We are saved by grace as well as works. The word of the Lord clearly states: **"For we labor diligently to write, to persuade our children, and also our brethren, to believe in Christ, and to be reconciled to God; for we know that it is *by grace that we are saved, after all we can do*"** (2 Nephi 25:23, italics added). We are saved by grace, for without the Atonement of Jesus Christ, we would indeed be lost. But we must also do our part. However, no one can be saved by works alone. However, the gift of salvation will not be given to someone who halfway obeys the commandments. How could we expect to inherit the kingdom of God with Abraham, Isaac, and Jacob, and all the righteous saints of the past, without our best effort? If salvation were achieved willy-nilly, with a few half-hearted acts of kindness, how prized would it be? On the other hand, does God require that we be exactly alike to achieve salvation? Does he require more than we are capable of doing?

What can we learn from the parable of the talents? Five talents were given to one man, two to another, and one to a third man, "according to his several ability." The men who received the five and the two doubled their talents, from five to ten and from two to four. These men were not exactly alike, but they both did their best. Therefore, both received the same reward: "Well done, good and faithful servant: thou hast been faithful over a few things, I will make thee ruler over many things: enter thou into the joy of thy lord" (Matthew 25:21, 23).

But what happened to the man who buried the one talent he had received?

> Then he which had received the one talent came and said, Lord, I knew that thou art an hard man, reaping where thou hast not sown, and gathering where thou hast not strawed: And I was afraid, and went and hid thy talent in the earth: lo, there thou hast that is thine. His lord answered and said unto him, Thou wicked and slothful servant, thou knewest that I reap where I sowed not, and gather where I have not strawed: Thou oughtest therefore to have put my money to the exchangers, and then at my coming I should have received mine own with usury. Take therefore the talent from him, and give

it unto him which hath ten talents. For unto every one that hath shall be given, and he shall have abundance: but from him that hath not shall be taken away even that which he hath. And cast ye the unprofitable servant into outer darkness: there shall be weeping and gnashing of teeth. (Matthew 25:24–30).

This parable sounds very much like the Book of Mormon reference quoted above: "**It is by grace that we are saved, *after all we can do***" (2 Nephi 25:23, italics added). Every one of us needs the grace of God or we will come up short in our efforts to obtain salvation in the kingdom of God.

In the last chapter of the Book of Mormon, Moroni gives his last exhortation:

> **I would exhort you that ye would come unto Christ, and lay hold upon every good gift, and touch not the evil gift, nor the unclean thing. . . . Yea, come unto Christ, and be perfected in him, and deny yourselves of all ungodliness; and if ye shall deny yourselves of all ungodliness, and love God with all your might, mind and strength, then is his *grace* sufficient for you, that by his *grace* ye may be perfect in Christ; and if by the *grace* of God ye are perfect in Christ, ye can in nowise deny the power of God. And again, if ye by the *grace* of God are perfect in Christ, and deny not his power, then are ye sanctified in Christ by the *grace* of God, through the shedding of the blood of Christ, which is in the covenant of the Father unto the remission of your sins, that ye become holy, without spot.** (Moroni 10:30, 32–33, italics added).

The Book of Mormon is "**the most correct of any book on earth**" (Introduction to the Book of Mormon).

Notes

1. Boyd K. Packer, "The things of my soul," *Ensign*, May 1986, 59.
2. Bruce R. McConkie, *A New Witness for the Articles of Faith* (Salt Lake City: Deseret Book, 1985), 460–461.

❦ 8 ❧

INTEGRITY OF THE BOOK OF MORMON WITH THE BIBLE

Those who claim that Joseph Smith wrote—rather than translated—the Book of Mormon would have to believe that Joseph Smith knew the Bible perfectly, especially the Old Testament, because there are no inconsistencies between the two records. On the contrary, Joseph Smith was not a Bible scholar. Yet the Bible and the Book of Mormon agree on history as well as on major points of doctrine. Volumes could be written showing how the Bible and Book of Mormon agree.

As I have studied both the Bible and the Book of Mormon, I have come to the conclusion that the Author of the Bible is also the Author of the Book of Mormon. In other words, both books came from the same Divine Source, namely the Lord, as revealed to holy prophets. In fact, the Book of Mormon is a witness to the veracity of the Bible. Although we acknowledge that the Bible is not perfect— for we believe it is true, "as far as it is translated correctly" (Article of Faith 1:8)—we do accept the vast majority of the Bible as being "translated correctly."

I shall briefly show how the Bible and Book of Mormon

agree completely on two important concepts and how the Book of Mormon actually amplifies our understanding of them:

THE SCATTERING AND GATHERING OF ISRAEL

If you are not a member of The Church of Jesus Christ of Latter-day Saints, I would be surprised if you are aware of this significantly important concept. The Prophet Moses exhorted Israel that when they entered the Promised Land, to obey the commandments and be an exemplary nation. However, he prophesied that after many generations they would serve idols, and if they did not repent, "the Lord shall scatter you among the nations . . . there ye shall serve gods, the work of men's hands . . . in the latter days, if thou turn unto the Lord thy God . . . he will not forsake thee . . . nor forget the covenant of thy fathers which he sware unto them" (Deuteronomy 4:27–31). "The Lord shall scatter thee among all people, from the one end of the earth even unto the other" (Deuteronomy 28:64). Ezekiel prophesied of the gathering: "I will accept you . . . when I bring you out from the people, and gather you out of the countries wherein ye have been scattered" (Ezekiel 20:41). Likewise, the Prophet Amos warned Israel, "I will sift the house of Israel among all nations," and then promised, "In that day will I raise up the tabernacle of David . . . as in the days of old" (Amos 9:9–11).

During the Savior's ministry, He tried to gather Israel. Said He, "I am not sent but unto the lost sheep of the house of Israel," but they rejected their Shepherd. The Prophet Jeremiah prophesied: "Hear the word of the Lord . . . He that scattered Israel will gather him, and keep him, as a shepherd doth his flock" (Jeremiah 31:10; see also Ezekiel 34:12).

Inasmuch as the Savior was rejected in the Meridian of time, Jeremiah's prophecy that the shepherd would "gather" Israel must apply to the latter days. The Prophet Isaiah spoke of the latter-day gathering when he prophesied: "He will lift up an ensign to the nations from far, and will hiss unto them from the end of the earth: and, behold, they shall come with speed swiftly" (Isaiah 5:26).

In addition to teaching about the scattering and gathering of Israel, the Book of Mormon explains that the scattering and gathering are an important part of God's efforts to save as many of His children as possible. Nephi explained that

> **The house of Israel . . . will be scattered upon all the face of the earth . . . and be confounded, because of the Holy One of Israel; for against him will they harden their hearts; wherefore, they shall be scattered among all nations and shall be hated of all men. . . . Wherefore, he will bring them again out of captivity, and they shall be gathered together . . . and they shall know that the Lord is their Savior and their Redeemer, the Mighty One of Israel. . . . And he gathereth his children from the four quarters of the earth; and he numbereth his sheep, and they know him; and there shall be one fold and one shepherd; . . . and in him they shall find pasture. (1 Nephi 22:3, 5, 12, 25).**

The Prophet Isaiah in the Bible, and as quoted in the Book of Mormon declared, **"And it shall come to pass in that day that the Lord shall set his hand again the second time to recover the remnant of his people. . . . And he shall set up an ensign for the nations, and shall assemble the outcasts of Israel, and gather together the dispersed of Judah from the four corners of the earth"** (2 Nephi 21:11–12; see also Isaiah 11:11–12).

The "first time" was when the Savior tried to gather

Israel during his mortal ministry; Jesus was rejected and cru-cified. The phrase **"the Lord set his hand again the second time,"** refers to the latter days with the coming forth of the Book of Mormon and the restoration of the true gospel of Jesus Christ.

What was the purpose of the gathering? Although the meaning is somewhat obscure in the Bible, it is crystal clear in the Book of Mormon: **"And after the house of Israel should be scattered they should be gathered together again . . . or come to the knowledge of the true Messiah, their Lord and their Redeemer"** (1 Nephi 10:14).

Several weeks after the completion of this chapter, as I was reading sequentially through the Book of Mormon, I read 3 Nephi 20:13, which says, **"Then shall the rem-nants, which shall be scattered abroad upon the face of the earth, be gathered in from the east and from the west, and from the south and from the north; and they shall be brought to the knowledge of the Lord their God, who hath redeemed them."** This verse defines the meaning of the "gathering of Israel," so I wanted to make sure that it was in my manuscript. I looked through the manuscript and found this place with the same definition in 1 Nephi 10:14. This is the way the Book of Mormon is. It is totally consistent from beginning to end. These two verses are not even cross-referenced, because those who created the cross-references missed a beautiful one. Here is another evidence that the author is the Lord Jesus Christ, not a mortal.

The Book of Mormon gives us a "sign" so we would know when the gathering commenced:

> **"And verily I say unto you, I give unto you a sign, that ye may know the time when these things shall be about to take place—that I shall gather in, from their long dispersion, my people, O house of Israel,**

and shall establish again among them my Zion; And behold, this is the thing which I will give unto you for a sign—for verily I say unto you that when these things [the Book of Mormon] . . . shall be made known unto the Gentiles . . . concerning this my people who shall be scattered by them; Verily, verily, I say unto you, when these things [the Book of Mormon] shall be made known unto them of the Father . . . for it is wisdom in the Father that they should be established in this land . . . by the power of the Father, that these things [the Book of Mormon] might come forth from them unto a remnant of your seed . . . it shall be a sign unto them, that . . . the work of the Father hath already commenced unto the fulfilling of the covenant which he hath made unto . . . the House of Israel. (3 Nephi 21:1–4, 7)

Thus, with the publishing of the Book of Mormon in 1830, the latter-day gathering began, and the Book of Mormon is a primary tool used in gathering the dispersed of Israel.

Thus, the Savior teaches us through the Book of Mormon that although he was rejected in the meridian of time, he had a plan in the last days— because of His loving kindness—to recover the remnants of the house of Israel as well as the Gentiles and all the inhabitants of the earth who would come unto Him.

THE LAW OF MOSES

The law of Moses refers to the whole host of written laws given through Moses to the children of Israel because of their inability to live the higher law. It "consisted of many ceremonies, rituals, and symbols, to remind the people frequently of their duties and responsibilities. It included a law of carnal commandments and performances."[1] Although the

Bible contains hundreds of references to the law of Moses, it fails to provide us with a full understanding of its purpose and how long it was to be lived.

The Book of Mormon prophets also commanded the people to live according to the law of Moses; however, the Book of Mormon gives a fuller understanding of the law than is presented in the Bible. **"They did keep the law of Moses. . . . But notwithstanding the law of Moses, they did look forward to the coming of Christ, considering that the law of Moses was a type of his coming. . . . Now they did not suppose that salvation came by the law of Moses; but the law of Moses did serve to strengthen their faith in Christ"** (Alma 25:15–16).

The Book of Mormon explains that the law of Moses was to be lived until it was fulfilled: **"Therefore, it is expedient that there should be a great and last sacrifice, and then shall there be, or it is expedient there should be, a stop to the shedding of blood; then shall the law of Moses be fulfilled . . . this is the whole meaning of the law, every whit pointing to that great and last sacrifice; and that great and last sacrifice will be the Son of God"** (Alma 34:13–14).

When the resurrected Christ appeared among the Nephites, he announced that the law of Moses was fulfilled: **"Behold, I am he that gave the law, and I am he who covenanted with my people Israel; therefore, the law in me is fulfilled, for I have come to fulfill the law; therefore it hath an end . . . the law which was given unto Moses hath an end in me. Behold, I am the law, and the light. Look unto me, and endure to the end, and ye shall live; for unto him that endureth to the end will I give eternal life"** (3 Nephi 15:5, 8–9).

Thanks to the Book of Mormon, it is now clear that the

law of Moses was a lesser law to help bring God's children to a better understanding of the life and Atonement of his Son Jesus Christ. The law of Moses, with its many sacrifices, pointed to the great and last sacrifice, which was the Son of God. The Atonement of Jesus Christ fulfilled or completed the law of Moses and put a stop to the shedding of blood. Now, it is easy to understand why the law of Moses was ended. It was fulfilled; it had completed its purpose.

It seems highly improbable that young Joseph Smith or anyone else in the 1820's could have written a book that is so completely compatible with the history and doctrine taught in the Bible, and yet adds so much to our understanding. Would you like to give Joseph Smith credit for explaining the truths explained in the Book of Mormon about grace and works and the scattering and gathering of Israel, or should we give credit to the Lord through the Book of Mormon prophets? Joseph Smith was not the originator of these truths, but the translator of a very sacred and ancient record that was preserved on gold plates.

Note
1. "The Law of Moses," Bible Dictionary, 722.

9

"GOD'S OWN HANDWRITING"

While working for the Church Curriculum Department, Roger Petersen, a coworker, and I made an amazing discovery. We were asked to help prepare footnotes for non-English editions of the Book of Mormon. We used the computer to look up every footnote in the English Book of Mormon, many of which cross-referenced to the Bible. We were to help identify footnotes that are based on principles. In the English KJV of the Bible, a significant number of footnotes are based on words only. Many of these "word" based footnotes would not work in non-English languages, because translation is *not* done word for word. Therefore, our job was to identify principle-based footnotes for inclusion in non-English editions of the Book of Mormon. As we looked for word phrases that are repeated in the scriptures we had a powerful spiritual experience. We discovered "God's own handwriting"—that is, hundreds of scriptural phrases that occur repeatedly in the Bible as well as in the Book of Mormon.

A phrase that was enlightening to me was "**thoughts and intents of the heart.**" Usually, we think of "thoughts" coming from the mind rather than the heart. Apparently

God is quite concerned with the "thoughts" of our hearts. Using the computer, we found the phrase, "thoughts and intents of the heart" in Hebrews 4:12 and three times in the Book of Mormon. (Note: By printing the verses from the Bible in regular type, and the verses from the Book of Mormon in bold, it is not my intent to demean the Bible, but to follow the format established at the first of this book of printing all quotes from the Book of Mormon in bold.)

In Hebrews 4:12, it reads: "For the word of God is quick, and powerful, and sharper than a two-edged sword, piercing even to the dividing asunder of soul and spirit, and of the joints and marrow, and is a discerner of the *thoughts and intents of the heart.*"

This phrase is also found in Mosiah 5:13, "**For how knoweth a man the master whom he has not served, . . . and is far from the *thoughts and intents of his heart?*"**; in Alma 12:7, "**Zeezrom began to tremble more exceedingly, for he was convinced more and more of the power of God; and he was also convinced that Alma and Amulek had a knowledge of him, for he was convinced that they knew the *thoughts and intents of his heart*; for power was given unto them that they might know of these things**"; and in Alma 18:32, "**And Ammon said: Yea, and he looketh down upon all the children of men; and he knows all the *thoughts and intents of the heart*; for by his hand were they all created from the beginning**" (italics added).

At the end of our assignment to identify principle-based footnotes, we had a list of phrases (examples of "God's own handwriting") that was forty pages long, and we believe there are more yet to be discovered. This was a tremendous testimony to us that all scripture is from the same Source, and that there is absolutely no way Joseph Smith or any other mortal could have written the Book of Mormon. The discovery of "God's own handwriting" is a witness of God's existence and of his continuous revelation to prophets.

Our findings corroborate the following statement by the Prophet Joseph Smith:

> The heavens declare the glory of God, and the firmament showeth His handiwork; and a moment's reflection is sufficient to teach every man of common intelligence, that all these are not the mere productions of chance. . . . He that can mark the power of Omnipotence, inscribed upon the heavens, can also see *God's own handwriting* in the sacred volume and he who reads it oftenest will like it best, and he who is acquainted with it, will know the hand wherever he can see it.[1]

I know by the power of the Holy Ghost that this statement is true!

Our findings also concur with the following statement by Elder Neal A. Maxwell: "One of the striking findings for the student of the scriptures is the frequency with which the same truth, the same idea, the same insight, the same principle appears (and often with exactly the same words) in various books of scripture. This is true not only with major doctrines, but also with very minor things that witness to the fact that the doctrines and truths that reappear come *from the same Source*" (italics added).[2]

I will share two more examples of *God's own handwriting*, and then provide a partial list of some of the more interesting ones we found. Under the inspiration of the Lord, the apostle Paul counseled the Corinthian saints: "Wherefore *come out from among them*, and *be ye separate*, saith the Lord, and *touch not the unclean thing*; and I will receive you" (2 Corinthians 6:17, italics added). In Zarahemla the inspired prophet Alma told the saints, "**And now I say unto you,**

all you that are desirous to follow the voice of the good Shepard, *come ye out from the wicked,* **and** *be ye separate,* **and** *touch not their unclean things*" (Alma 5:57, italics added).

The next example is probably the most extensive one we discovered. In 1 John 3:1–3, John wrote, "Behold, what manner of *love* the Father hath *bestowed upon* us, that we should be called *the sons of God*: therefore the world knoweth us not, because it knew him not. Beloved, now are we *the sons of God,* and it doth not yet appear what we shall be: but we know that, *when he shall appear, we shall be like him; for we shall see him as he is.* And every man that *hath this hope in him purifieth himself, even as he is pure*" (italics added).

Compare this beautiful message with the conclusion of Mormon's inspiring talk on faith, hope and charity: **"Wherefore, my beloved brethren, pray unto the Father with all the energy of heart, that ye may be filled with this** *love,* **which he hath** *bestowed upon* **all who are true followers of his Son, Jesus Christ; that ye may become** *the sons of God*; **that** *when he shall appear we shall be like him, for we shall see him as he is*; **that we may** *have this hope; that we may be purified even as he is pure.* **Amen"** (Moroni 7:48, italics added).

These phrases are excerpted from longer passages and ought to be studied in context because they are part of beautiful messages. These messages flow so naturally that one would probably not notice the phrase until it is pointed out or shows up when using the computer.

Following are a few of the more interesting examples of "God's own handwriting". (I will give only one reference from the Bible and one from the Book of Mormon. When the Bible or Book of Mormon have more than one reference it is so indicated in parenthesis.)

"**a more excellent way**" 1 Corinthians 12:31; Ether 12:11

"**altar of stones**" (Not "stone altar") Deuteronomy 27:5; 1 Nephi 2:7

"**anchor of the soul**" Hebrews 6:19; Ether 12:4

"**as the Lord liveth**" (said as an oath in making a covenant) Ruth 3:13; 1 Nephi 3:15 (This phrase is repeated many times in both the Bible and the Book of Mormon.)

"**as a hen gathereth her chickens under her wings**" Matthew 23:37; 3 Nephi 10:4–6 (Bible–2)

"**as a young lion among the flocks of sheep**" Micah 5:8; 3 Nephi 21:12

"**author and finisher of their faith**" Hebrews 12:2; Moroni 6:4

"**cleave unto every good thing**" Romans 12:9; Moroni 7:28

"**driven about as chaff before the wind**" Psalm 1:4; Mormon 5:16 (Bible–2)

"**elements shall melt with fervent heat**" 2 Peter 3:10; Mormon 9:2 (Book of Mormon–2)

"**eye single**" Matthew 6:22; Mormon 8:15

"**fiery darts of the adversary**" Ephesians 6:16; 1 Nephi 15:24

"**from the foundation of the world**" Revelation 13:8; Mosiah 4:6–7 (Bible–5; Book of Mormon–4.)

"**garments were washed white through the blood of the

Lamb" Revelation 7:14; Alma 13:11 (Book of Mormon–6)

"**gates of hell**" Matthew 16:18; 3 Nephi 18:13 (Book of Mormon–3)

"**hardness of heart**" Mark 16:14; Ether 4:15 (Bible–2; Book of Mormon–4)

"**land of promise**" Hebrews 11:9; Jacob 2:12 (Bible–2; Book of Mormon–at least 7)

"**led by the Spirit**" Luke 4:1; 1 Nephi 4:6 (Bible–2; Book of Mormon–5)

"**my grace is sufficient**" 2 Corinthians 12:9; Ether 12:26–27 (Book of Mormon–2)

"**my Spirit will not always strive with man**" Genesis 6:3; Ether 2:15 (Book of Mormon–4)

"**nations, kindreds, tongues, and people**" Revelation 7:9; 1 Nephi 11:36 (Book of Mormon–more than 3)

"**perfect love casteth out all fear**" 1 John 4:18; Moroni 8:16

"**speak unto them out of the ground, and their speech shall be low out of the dust, and their voice shall be as one that hath a familiar spirit . . . that he may whisper concerning them, even as it were out of the ground; and their speech shall whisper out of the dust.**" Isaiah 29:4; 2 Nephi 26:16 (Book of Mormon–7)

"**Spirit is the same, yesterday, today, and forever**" Hebrews 13:8; 2 Nephi 2:4 (Book of Mormon–6)

"**stay his hand**" Daniel 4:35; Moroni 9:14

"**still small voice**" 1 Kings 19:12; 1 Nephi 17:45

"**their works do follow them**" Revelation 14:13; 3 Nephi 27:12

"**there are they who were first, who shall be last; and there are they who were last, who shall be first**" Luke 13:30; Ether 13:12

"**these signs shall follow them that believe**" Mark 16:17; Mormon 9:24 (Book of Mormon–2)

"**thrust in the sickle**" Revelation 14:15; Alma 26:5

"**time is at hand**" Matthew 26:18; Alma 5:31 (Bible–2; Book of Mormon–2)

"**treasure in heaven**" Luke 18:22; Helaman 5:8 (Bible–3)

"**without the walls**" Jeremiah 21:4; 1 Nephi 4:24 (Bible–2; Book of Mormon–3)

"**word of God, which is quick and powerful**" Hebrews 4:12; Helaman 3:29 (Bible–2)

"*__work out your own salvation with fear and trembling__*" Phillipians 2:12; Mormon 9:27

There are many more examples of similar phrases in the Bible and Book of Mormon. These similarities are evidence that God speaks through his chosen prophets. Prophets speak the word of the Lord in their own language, but they often give the word of God directly. Isaiah and Jeremiah both recorded the following from the Lord: "I have put my words in thy mouth" (see Isaiah 51:16 and Jeremiah 1:9). When Moses was called to be a prophet, he was concerned because he was slow of speech. The Lord told him, "I will be with thy mouth, and teach thee what thou shalt say" (Exodus 4:12). In his final testimony Nephi declared, "**These words . . . are**

the words of Christ, and he hath given them unto me" (2 Nephi 33:10).

The Bible contains the word of God revealed to prophets who recorded his words. The original manuscripts were copied over and over by scribes and were translated into many languages. The scribes and translators made errors, but for the most part did an incredible job preserving the word of the Lord. The Book of Mormon is the word of God recorded on gold plates and translated into English by a prophet under the inspiration of God. Joseph Smith could not have written the inspiring passages within this marvelous record. The Book of Mormon and the Bible contain the sacred word of God. It was a marvelous experience to discover "God's own handwriting" in these books. To proclaim Joseph Smith or some other person as the author of the Book of Mormon would be acknowledging him as an inspired literary genius with a perfect knowledge of the Bible.

Notes

1. *Teachings of the Prophet Joseph Smith* (Salt Lake City: Deseret Book, 1976), 56, italics added.
2. Neal A Maxwell, *Things as They Really Are* (Salt Lake City: Shadow Mountain, 1989), 84–85.

10

ISAIAH PASSAGES IN THE BOOK OF MORMON

After Lehi's family escaped from Jerusalem in about 600 BC, Lehi was commanded by the Lord to send his sons back to Jerusalem to obtain the Plates of Brass. When Lehi's sons returned, Lehi searched these plates and found that they contained "**the prophecies of the holy prophets, from the beginning, even down to the commencement of the reign of Zedekiah**" (1 Nephi 5:10–13). Zedekiah's reign commenced in 600 BC. Isaiah prophesied in Jerusalem around 740 BC, and so as would be expected, the Plates of Brass contained the prophecies of Isaiah. Nephi was a student of the scriptures, and he loved the words of Isaiah. Nephi used Isaiah's words to try to help his wayward brothers understand what Lehi had taught them about the natural branches of the olive tree and the Gentiles. "**I did rehearse unto them the words of Isaiah, who spake concerning the restoration of the . . . house of Israel**" (1 Nephi 15:20).

Later, when Nephi was trying to help his brothers believe in the Savior, he said, "**That I might more fully persuade them to believe in the Lord their Redeemer I did read** unto them that which was written by the prophet Isaiah" (1 Nephi 19:23).

In 2 Nephi 11, Nephi tells us his feelings about Isaiah's words. "**And now I, Nephi, write more of the words of Isaiah, for my soul delighteth in his words . . . for he verily saw my Redeemer, even as I have seen him. And my brother, Jacob, also has seen him as I have seen him; wherefore, I will send their words forth unto my children to *prove* unto them that my words are true**" (2 Nephi 11:2–3, italics added).

Here, Nephi used the law of witnesses: "**Wherefore, by the words of three, God hath said, I will establish my word. . . . Behold, my soul delighteth in *proving* unto my people the truth of the coming of Christ**" (2 Nephi 11:3–4, italics added). Then, Nephi recorded twelve chapters of Isaiah. (See 2 Nephi 12–24 which correspond to Isaiah 2–14.)

When critics first learn that there are whole chapters of Isaiah in the Book of Mormon, they may be tempted to ignorantly claim that Joseph Smith copied these chapters from the King James Version of the Bible. However, closer scrutiny of these chapters reveals a powerful witness that the Book of Mormon is in reality one of the best, if not the best, commentary on the book of Isaiah in existence.

Isaiah recorded his prophesies around 740 BC. The earliest manuscripts for Isaiah in the KJV are dated around 200 BC. Book of Mormon prophets used the Plates of Brass as their source for the writings of Isaiah. The Plates of Brass were written prior to 600 BC, hundreds of years before the manuscripts used in creating the KJV. Therefore, one who accepts the divine origin of the Book of Mormon should expect to find that the Isaiah passages in the Book of Mormon are more accurate than those in the KJV. And indeed they are! Footnote 2a in 2 Nephi 12 reads:

"**Comparison with the King James Bible in English shows that there are differences in more than half of the 433 verses of Isaiah quoted in the Book of Mormon, while about 200 verses have the same wording as KJV.**" A careful comparison of the verses where there are differences reveals some amazing discoveries that help in better understanding Isaiah. Several authors have written books about the Isaiah passages in the Book of Mormon. My purpose is to briefly explain a few comparisons that especially impress me.

One of the most striking discoveries I made when carefully comparing Isaiah passages in the Book of Mormon with corresponding passages in the KJV had to do with the word *not*. There are several verses where the word *not* is found in the Book of Mormon, but not in the KJV, or vice versa. Of course, to add or delete the word *not* completely reverses the meaning. One of the more striking examples is found by comparing Isaiah 2:9 with 2 Nephi 12:9. The word *not* appears three times in the 2 Nephi passage and only once in the KJV.

Isaiah 2:9	*2 Nephi 12:9*
And the mean man boweth down, and the great man humbleth himself: therefore forgive them *not*.	**And the mean man boweth *not* down, and the great man humbleth himself *not*, therefore, forgive him *not*.**

A careful reading of these verses in context reveals that the Book of Mormon passage makes much more sense. In

Isaiah 2, the prophet is speaking of the latter days, just before the Second Coming. It is a time of great wickedness as Isaiah explains in verse 8: "Their land is also full of idols; they worship the work of their own hands, that which their own fingers have made." When you analyze Isaiah 2:9, it does not make sense. Why would you not forgive a mean man who bows down or a great man who humbles himself? 2 Nephi 12:9 is much more believable.

For other examples compare Isaiah 48:2 with 1 Nephi 20:2 and Isaiah 9:3 with 2 Nephi 19:3. Following is an example where the word *not* is not in the KJV, but is in 2 Nephi. Compare Isaiah 3:6 with 2 Nephi 13:6. Which verse seems to be more accurate? Another enlightening comparison is between Isaiah 3:9 and 2 Nephi 13:9. Here again the Book of Mormon passage makes more sense than the Isaiah passage. In Isaiah it says, "They declare their sin as Sodom, they hide it not. Woe unto their soul! For they have rewarded evil unto themselves." Whereas in 2 Nephi it reads: "**. . . doth declare their sin to be even as Sodom, and they cannot hide it. Wo unto their souls, for they have rewarded evil unto themselves!**" The Isaiah passage suggests that they *could* hide their sin, whereas the Book of Mormon says they *cannot* hide their sin.

It is very enlightening to make a side-by-side comparison of the Isaiah passages in the Book of Mormon with their corresponding passages in Isaiah in the Old Testament. The Book of Mormon forthrightly challenges both scholar and the humblest reader to "compare" the Isaiah passages between both texts. Following is a list of major Isaiah passages in the Book of Mormon with their corresponding passages in Isaiah:

1 Nephi 20–21	Isaiah 48–49
2 Nephi 7–8	Isaiah 50–51 and 52:1–2
2 Nephi 12–24	Isaiah 2–14
2 Nephi 27	Isaiah 29
Mosiah 14	Isaiah 53
3 Nephi 22	Isaiah 54

As stated earlier, the Book of Mormon is an extremely valuable commentary on Isaiah. A study of the surrounding Book of Mormon chapters of those listed above is a tremendous aid to one's increased understanding of Isaiah. For example, after quoting Isaiah 2–14, Nephi writes, "**Now I, Nephi, do speak somewhat concerning the words which I have written, which have been spoken by the mouth of Isaiah**" (2 Nephi 25:1). Then, Nephi proceeds to give valuable insight into the words of Isaiah. An insightful comment by Nephi regarding Isaiah's words is that "**They shall be of great worth unto them in the last days; for in that day shall they understand them**" (2 Nephi 25:8). Couple this statement with what the Resurrected Christ said after quoting Isaiah 54 to the people in America when He visited them, "**And now, behold, I say unto you, that ye ought to search these things. Yea, a commandment I give unto you that ye search these things diligently; for great are the words of Isaiah. For surely he spake as touching all things concerning my people which are of the house of Israel. . . . And all things that he spake have been and shall be, even according to the words which he spake**" (3 Nephi 23:1–3).

If one believes Joseph Smith wrote the Book of Mormon, Joseph gets credit for correcting Isaiah in the Old Testament. However, if Joseph Smith translated the Book of Mormon from an ancient record, the recorder of the Plates of Brass evidently had an earlier source that was more accurate than the source used by the compilers of the KJV.

The book *Isaiah in the Book of Mormon*, edited by Donald W. Parry and John W. Welch, contains nineteen essays by LDS scholars who take a variety of approaches in helping us better understand the amazing prophecies of Isaiah included in the Book of Mormon.

If a twenty-four-year-old, unschooled, young man in 1829 were to write a fraudulent narrative about the religious history of ancient America, would you expect to find within its pages extensive quotations from Isaiah which actually clarify the writings of that great prophet?

❧ 11 ❧

CHIASMUS

Chiasmus is an interesting literary device. The form in Hebrew dates at least to the eighth or tenth centuries BC in Isaiah and in the Psalms, before the time of Lehi and Nephi (600 BC).

> The name chiasmus . . . was derived from chi (X), the twenty-second letter in the Greek alphabet, and the Greek *chiazein* (to mark with an X). . . . Two lines of poetry are said to be parallel if the component elements of one line correspond directly to those of the other . . . e.g.
>
> A soft answer turneth away wrath:
> But grievous words stir up anger.
> (Proverbs 15:1)
>
> If the second line of a parallelism is inverted, that is to say, if its last element is placed first and the first, last, then a chiasm is created. The following is an example of chiasmus:
>
> For *my* thoughts are not *your* thoughts
> Neither are *your* ways *my* ways, saith the Lord.
> (Isaiah 55:8)[1]

A chiasm is a repetition of ideas in inverted order. The

simplest chiasm contains four elements and can be diagramed in the form of an X:

$$A \diagdown B$$
$$B \diagup A$$

An example of this simple chiasm from the Savior's words in the New Testament is as follows:

A "But many that are *first*
  B shall be *last*;
  B¹ and the *last*
A¹ shall be *first*." (Matthew 19:30)[2]

A chiasm "may be expanded to include any number of terms written in one order and then in exact reverse order, such as:

$$A\text{-}B\text{-}C\text{-}D\text{-} \ldots \text{-}X\text{-}X\text{-} \ldots \text{-}D\text{-}C\text{-}B\text{-}A\text{"}[3]$$

In the above example, the double X's represent the center or turning point. The center often contains the main idea or teaching the chiasm was designed to teach. Many more complicated chiasms have been discovered in the Bible and may be several verses or several chapters long.

Knowledge of chiasmus in the Bible was lost for centuries and was rediscovered in England in the 1820s. With the publication of Horne's *Introduction to the Critical Study and Knowledge of the Holy Scriptures* (1825) and *The Symmetrical Structures of Scripture* by John Forbes in 1854 in Scotland, serious Bible students began to learn about chiasmus in the Bible. However, it is doubtful Joseph Smith or anyone else in America knew about chiasmus prior to 1830. The Book of Mormon had been published and read by millions for more than 130 years before chiasmus was discovered in the Book of Mormon by John W. Welch, a young missionary in 1967.

In other words chiasmus was inscribed by the original Nephite record keepers. Joseph Smith translated the Book of Mormon from the Plates of Mormon and was probably unaware of the presence of chiasmus in the Book of Mormon.

John Welch gives nine examples of chiasmus in 1 and 2 Nephi, Mosiah, and Alma and indicates that others may be found throughout the Book of Mormon. Following are two amazing examples of chiasmus in the Book of Mormon. (How could anyone honestly or logically believe that Joseph Smith or anyone else in the early 1800s created these beautiful examples of chiasmus?)

And now whosoever shall not take upon them the *name of Christ*
    must be *called* by some other name;
      therefore he findeth himself on the *left hand of God.*
        And I would that ye should *remember* that this is the name
            that should never be *blotted out*
              except it be through *transgression;*
              therefore
              take heed that ye do not *transgress*
            that the name be not *blotted* out of your hearts.
        I would that ye should *remember* to retain this name
      that ye are not found on the *left hand of God,*
    but that ye hear and know the voice by which ye shall be *called*
and also the *name* by which he shall call you. (Mosiah 5:10–12)[4]

Alma 36

My son give ear to my words (v. 1)
  Keep the commandments and ye shall prosper in the land (v. 1)
    Captivity of our fathers—bondage (v. 2)
      He surely did deliver them (v. 2)
        Trust in God (v. 3)
          Support in trials, troubles, and afflictions (v. 3)
            I know this not of myself but of God (v. 4)
              Born of God (v. 5)
                Limbs paralysed (v. 10)

                  The Agony of Conversion
                    destroyed (v. 11)
                    racked with eternal torment (v. 12)
                    harrowed up to the greatest degree (v. 12)
                    racked with all my sins (v. 12)
                    tormented with the pains of hell (v. 13)
                    inexpressible horror (v. 14)
                    banished and extinct (v. 15)
                    pains of a damned soul (v. 16)

                      Called upon Jesus Christ

                  The Joy of Conversion
                    no more pain (v. 19)
                    oh what joy (v. 20)
                    what marvelous light (v. 20)
                    soul filled with joy as exceeding as was my pain
                      (v. 20)
                    exquisite (v. 21)
                    nothing as sweet as was my joy (v. 22)
                    singing and praising God (v. 22)
                    long to be with God (v. 22)

                Use of Limbs returns (v. 23)
                Born of God (v. 26)
             Therefore my knowledge is of God (v. 26)
          Supported under trials and troubles and afflictions (v. 27)
         Trust in him (v. 27)
      He will deliver me (v. 27)
    Egypt—captivity (v. 28–29)
  Keep the commandments and ye shall prosper in land (v. 30)
This according to his word (v. 30)[5]

For more information, see "What Does Chiasmus in the Book of Mormon Prove?" by John W. Welch published in *Book of Mormon Authorship Revisited* edited by Noel B. Reynolds (1997 Foundation for Ancient Research and Mormon Studies).

notes
1. John W. Welch, *BYU Studies*, 10:1 (Autumn 1969): 69–70.
2. http://en.wikipedia.org/wiki/Chiasmus
3. John W. Welch, *BYU Studies*, 10:1 (Autumn 1969), 71.
4. Ibid, 77.
5. Ibid, 83.

12

HEBRAISMS

The original record keepers of the Book of Mormon engraved their words on golden plates. The task of engraving on metal must have been laborious. What could a record keeper do if he made an engraving mistake? He could not erase his error. Careful study of the Book of Mormon reveals a possible answer. See if you can discover a method that appears to have been used to correct an engraving error by studying Alma 24:19 and Alma 43:38.

Have you figured it out? Alma 24 tells of a group of Lamanites who had been ferocious enemies of the Nephites who were converted to the gospel. As a token of their commitment to never take the life of another, they buried their weapons. The Book of Mormon reads "**They buried their weapons of peace, OR they buried the weapons of war, for peace**" (Alma 24:19, emphasis added). Here it appears that the record keeper corrected his engraving mistake in stating "**weapons of peace**" by adding "**or they buried their weapons of war, for peace**."

In explaining why the Lamanites suffered more deaths

in hand-to-hand combat than the Nephites, the record states:

> **The work of death commenced on both sides, but it was more dreadful on the part of the Lamanites, for their nakedness was exposed to the heavy blows of the Nephites with their swords and their cimiters, which brought death almost at every stroke. While on the other hand, there was now and then a man fell among the Nephites, by their swords and the loss of blood, they being shielded from the more vital parts of the body, OR the more vital parts of the body being shielded from the strokes of the Lamanites, by their breastplates, and their armshields, and their head-plates.** (Alma 43:37–38, emphasis added).

Notice how the word *or* was apparently used to correct what was first engraved: "**being shielded from the more vital parts of the body.**"

Other apparent examples of the use of *or* to correct an engraving error are found in the following references, and there are likely others yet to be discovered: Mosiah 22:6; Alma 53:10; Alma 57:8; Alma 59:3; Alma 61:8; Alma 63:15; and Helaman 11:24.

"If the Book of Mormon was really written by Nephi and other prophets familiar with Hebrew, we would expect the Hebrew form of thinking to frequently appear in their writing. And it does! The term scholars use when a Hebrew form of thinking or writing shows up in English is *Hebraism*, and the Book of Mormon is full of Hebraisms."[1] Chiasmus is the greatest example of Hebraism in the Book of Mormon. (See chapter 11.)

Consider the following additional examples:

1. "But behold, a hundredeth part of the proceedings of this people, yea, the account of the Lamanites AND of

the Nephites, AND their wars, AND contentions, AND dissensions, AND their preaching, AND their prophecies, AND their shipping AND their building of ships, AND their building of temples, AND of synagogues AND their sanctuaries, AND their righteousness, AND their wickedness, AND their murders, AND their robbings, AND their plundering, AND all manner of abominations AND whoredoms, cannot be contained in this work" (Helaman 3:14, emphasis added.) Why all the "ands?" Commas do not exist in Hebrew. Instead they use conjunctions like "and." In chapter 43 of Alma, thirty-four of the fifty-four verses start with the word *and*.

2. The Book of Mormon refers to the record Lehi and his sons brought from Jerusalem as the "**Brass Plates of Laban**" rather than "Laban's Brass Plates," and as the "**plates of brass**" rather than the "brass plates" (1 Nephi 4:24).

The Book of Mormon speaks of an "**altar of stones**" rather than a "stone altar" (1 Nephi 2:7); the "**servant of Laban**" and "**voice of Laban**" rather than "Laban's servant" or "Laban's voice" (1 Nephi 4:20); the "**voice of the Spirit**" rather than the "Spirit's voice" (1 Nephi 4:18); the "**rod of iron**" rather than the "iron rod" (1 Nephi 8:19); the "**love of God**" rather than "God's love" (1 Nephi 11:22); the "**Lamb of God**" instead of "God's Lamb" (1 Nephi 11:21); the "**word of God**" rather than "God's word" (1 Nephi 15:24); the "**gifts of God**" rather than "God's gifts" (1 Nephi 15:36); and the "**daughter of Ishmael**" rather than "Ishmael's daughter" (1 Nephi 16:7).

If you desire more examples, you may find them throughout the Book of Mormon. Why? Apostrophe "s" does not exist in Hebrew. "In Hebrew . . . when a noun is used to describe another noun, frequently the word *of* is used to connect them."[2]

3. Elder Jeffrey R. Holland, then of the Quorum of the Seventy, shared a Book of Mormon evidence that touched his heart as a young man:

> I can still remember the scriptural awakening that came to me when a skillful and well-prepared seminary teacher . . . asked me, in class, why in 1 Nephi 2:6 the Book of Mormon records that Lehi **"pitched his tent in a valley by the side of a river of water."** . . . Being the smart-aleck student I almost always was, I made a clever response about it being smarter to pitch a tent by the side of a river than in it . . . I knew I was a hit because the girls giggled.
>
> The teacher didn't giggle. He smiled and he said, with the smile still on his face, "You're not answering the question, Jeff, because you're not reading the text. It doesn't say that Lehi pitched his tent by the river or in the river; it says he pitched it by a river of water. Why did he say a **'river of water,'** Jeff? What other kinds of rivers are there, Jeff?"
>
> The young student didn't know what to say. What other kinds of rivers are there, anyway? His teacher went on to explain to the class that in the deserts of Arabia there are rivers of sand as well as rivers of water. Although you and I might have thought that the only kinds of rivers were rivers of water, Nephi knew different; therefore, he specified what kind of river it was. This short phrase, "river of water," provides simple evidence that the Book of Mormon was written by somebody familiar with Arabic geography. Joseph Smith was not![3]

4. "In Hebrew an *and* is used to connect compound numbers between twenty-one and ninety-nine. All numbers in the Book of Mormon use this Hebraic format."[4] Instead of saying the "thirty-eighth year," the Book of Mormon record keepers wrote the "**thirty and eighth year**" (Alma 63:7).

This manner of recording numbers is consistent throughout the Book of Mormon.

5. Following is another example of Hebraism in the Book of Mormon (it's lousy English, but good Hebrew):

- "**I and my brethren**" instead of "my brethren and I" (1 Nephi 3:10; 7:22; Alma 27:15)
- "**I and my father**" instead of "my father and I" (1 Nephi 5:20; 1 Nephi 22:31)
- "**I and the children**" instead of "the children and I" (2 Nephi 18:18)
- "**I and my people**" instead of "my people and I." (Mosiah 9:7, 16, 17; 11:27)

If Joseph Smith had written the Book of Mormon would he not have written "my brethren and I" and so on?

Notes

1. John Hilton, III, *Book of Mormon Evidences* (Salt Lake City: Deseret Book, 2007), 37.
2. Ibid, 38.
3. Ibid, 65–67.
4. Ibid, 42.

13

THE TESTIMONIES OF NEPHI AND MORONI

Near the end of his life, Nephi recorded his powerful testimony of the Savior and the record he had engraved upon gold plates:

The words which I have written in weakness . . . speaketh of Jesus, and persuadeth them to believe in him, and to endure to the end, which is life eternal. And it speaketh harshly against sin, according to the plainness of the truth; wherefore, no man will be angry at the words which I have written save he shall be of the spirit of the devil.

I glory in plainness; I glory in truth; I glory in my Jesus, for he hath redeemed my soul from hell. I have charity for my people, and great faith in Christ that I shall meet many souls spotless at his judgment-seat. I have charity for the Jew—I say Jew, because I mean them from whence I came. I also have charity for the Gentiles. But behold, for none of these can I hope except they shall be reconciled unto Christ, and enter into the narrow gate, and walk in the strait path which leads to life, and continue in the path until the end of the day of probation.

And now, my beloved brethren, and also Jew, and

all ye ends of the earth, hearken unto these words and believe in Christ; and if ye believe not in these words believe in Christ. And if ye shall believe in Christ ye will believe in these words, for *they are the words of Christ*, and he hath given them unto me; and they teach all men that they should do good. And if they are not the words of Christ, judge ye—for Christ will show unto you, with power and great glory, that they are his words, at the last day; and you and I shall stand face to face before his bar; and ye shall know that I have been commanded of him to write these things, notwithstanding my weakness.

And I pray the Father in the name of Christ that many of us, if not all, may be saved in his kingdom at that great and last day. And now, my beloved brethren, all those who are of the house of Israel, and all ye ends of the earth, I speak unto you as the voice of one crying from the dust: Farewell until that great day shall come. And you that will not partake of the goodness of God, and respect the words of the Jews, and also my words, and the words which shall proceed out of the mouth of the Lamb of God, behold, I bid you an everlasting farewell, for these words shall condemn you at the last day. For what I seal on earth, shall be brought against you at the judgment bar; for thus hath the Lord commanded me, and I must obey. Amen. (2 Nephi 33:4–15).

After abridging the twenty-four plates of Ether, Moroni, the last record keeper, concluded the twelfth chapter of Ether with his powerful testimony: "**And now I, Moroni, bid farewell . . . until we shall meet before the judgment-seat of Christ . . . And then shall ye know that I have seen Jesus, and that he hath talked with me face to face. . . . And now, I would commend you to seek this Jesus of whom the prophets and apostles have written, that the grace of**

God the Father, and also the Lord Jesus Christ, and the Holy Ghost, which beareth record of them, may be and abide in you forever. Amen" (Ether 12:38–39, 41).

Speaking of the day when the Book of Mormon would come forth, Moroni declared: "**It shall come in a day when it shall be said that miracles are done away; and it shall come even as if one should speak from the dead. . . . Behold, I speak unto you as if ye were present, and yet ye are not. But behold, Jesus Christ hath shown you unto me, and I know your doing**" (Mormon 8:26, 35).

Around AD 400, Moroni recorded the following:

> And whoso receiveth this record, and shall not condemn it because of the imperfections which are in it, the same shall know of greater things than these. Behold, I am Moroni; and were it possible, I would make all things known unto you. . . . I am the son of Mormon, and my father was a descendant of Nephi. I am the same who hideth up this record unto the Lord. . . . And if there be faults they be the faults of a man. But behold, we know no fault; nevertheless God knoweth all things; therefore, he that condemneth, let him be aware lest he shall be in danger of hell fire. (Mormon 8:12–14, 17)

Before burying the gold plates in the Hill Cumorah in about AD 421, Moroni engraved his final testimony:

> And when ye shall receive these things, I would exhort you that ye would ask God, the Eternal Father, in the name of Christ, if these things are not true; and if ye shall ask with a sincere heart, with real intent, having faith in Christ, he will manifest the truth of it unto you, by the power of the Holy Ghost. . . . And God shall show unto you, that what I have written is true. . . . I soon go to rest in the paradise of God, until my spirit and body shall again reunite, and I

**am brought forth triumphant through the air, to
meet you before the pleasing bar of the great Jeho-
vah, the Eternal Judge of both quick and dead. Amen.**
(Moroni 10:4, 29, 34)

How many others will be at the final judgment bar? The
Three and the Eight Witnesses? The Prophet Joseph Smith?
The inhabitants of ancient America who touched the prints
of the nails in the hands and feet of the resurrected Savior?
Thousands of men and women of the latter days who have
put Moroni's promise to the test?

On October 4, 2009, Elder Jeffrey R. Holland of the
Quorum of the Twelve Apostles bore a stirring testimony of
the Book of Mormon:

> I ask that my testimony of the Book of Mormon
> and all that it implies, given today under my own oath
> and office, be recorded by men on earth and angels in
> heaven. . . . I want it absolutely clear when I stand before
> the judgment bar of God that I declared to the world,
> in the most straightforward language I could summon,
> that the Book of Mormon is true, that it came forth the
> way Joseph said it came forth and was given to bring
> happiness and hope to the faithful in the travail of the
> latter days.[1]

Note

1. Jeffrey R. Holland, "Safety for the Soul," *Ensign,* Nov. 2009, 90.

CONCLUSION

To those of you who have completed your reading of this book, I thank you for taking the time to consider my findings. It has been a very fun and enjoyable experience for me to try to organize my thoughts. I hope they have been understandable.

It would be interesting for me to talk with you in person. I hope you have or will accept Moroni's challenge to read, ponder, and ask God in the name of Jesus Christ if the Book of Mormon is true. He will manifest its truthfulness unto you by the power of the Holy Ghost. I testify that if you make studying and pondering the words in this sacred record on a regular basis it will help you get nearer to God.

With Sincerity,
Tom G. Rose

ABOUT THE AUTHOR

Tom G. Rose was born in 1939 in Southern California. He attended early-morning seminary as a senior in high school and the next two years while attending San Bernardino Valley College. During his last year of seminary he obtained a strong spiritual testimony of the Book of Movrmon. The next summer he left for a 2½ year mission to North Western Mexico.

Following his mission he attended Brigham Young University and obtained a bachelor's degree with a secondary teaching certificate. He participated in training for prospective seminary teachers while at BYU and was hired to teach seminary in 1964 in Ogden, Utah. During the next seven years, he taught the Book of Mormon course each year. In

1969, Tom received a Master of Religious Education Degree from BYU. His major was religious education and his minor was Church history.

Tom was transferred to the Seminary Curriculum Department in 1970 where he helped write the first home study seminary course on the Book of Mormon. In 1975 Tom was invited to join the staff of the new Church Curriculum Department where he worked for twenty-one years as the supervisor of Child Curriculum Development. In addition to supervising the writing of the Primary lesson manuals, Tom had major input in the following projects that utilized his knowledge of the Book of Mormon:

> *Book of Mormon Stories*
> *Primary 4 Book of Mormon Ages 8-11*
> *Guide to the Scriptures*
> Footnotes for non-English editions of the
>   Book of Mormon
> Adult Book of Mormon courses

Tom estimates that he has read the Book of Mormon fifty to sixty times from cover to cover as part of his daily personal scripture study and as he taught and worked with curriculum development.

Tom and his wife, Marilyn, have eight children and thirty grandchildren. They reside in West Jordan, Utah, and are temple ordinance workers in the Jordan River Temple.